THE MATCH THAT BECOMES
A CONFLAGRATION

other books by the author

POETRY
Dawn Visions
Burnt Heart/Ode to the War Dead
This Body of Black Light Gone Through the Diamond
The Desert is the Only Way Out
The Chronicles of Akhira
The Blind Beekeeper
Mars & Beyond
Laughing Buddha Weeping Sufi
Salt Prayers
Ramadan Sonnets
Psalms for the Brokenhearted
I Imagine a Lion
Coattails of the Saint
Abdallah Jones and the Disappearing-Dust Caper (illustrated by the author)
Love is a Letter Burning in a High Wind
The Flame of Transformation Turns to Light
Underwater Galaxies
The Music Space
Cooked Oranges
Through Rose Colored Glasses
Like When You Wave at a Train and the Train Hoots Back at You
In the Realm of Neither
The Fire Eater's Lunchbreak
Millennial Prognostications
You Open a Door and it's a Starry Night
Where Death Goes
Shaking the Quicksilver Pool
The Perfect Orchestra
Sparrow on the Prophet's Tomb
A Maddening Disregard for the Passage of Time
Stretched Out on Amethysts
Invention of the Wheel
Sparks Off the Main Strike
Chants for the Beauty Feast
In Constant Incandescence
Holiday from the Perfect Crime
The Caged Bear Spies the Angel
The Puzzle
Ramadan is Burnished Sunlight
Ala-udeen & The Magic Lamp (illustrated by the author)
The Crown of Creation (illustrated by the author)
Blood Songs
Down at the Deep End (with drawings by the author)
Next Life
A Hundred Little 3D Pictures
He Comes Running (chapbook)
Miracle Songs for the Millennium
The Throne Perpendicular to All that is Horizontal
The Soul's Home
Some
Facing Mecca
Eternity Shimmers Time Holds its Breath
Stories Too Fiery to Sing Too Watery to Whisper
The Sweet Enigma of it All
The Sound of Geese Over the House
White Noise in This World Silver in the Next
The Match that Becomes a Conflagration

THEATER / THE FLOATING LOTUS MAGIC OPERA COMPANY
The Walls Are Running Blood / Bliss Apocalypse

THE MATCH THAT BECOMES A CONFLAGRATION

POEMS

OCTOBER 14, 2011 - MAY 9, 2012

DANIEL ABDAL-HAYY MOORE

THE ECSTATIC EXCHANGE
2016
PHILADELPHIA

The Match That Becomes a Conflagration
Copyright © 2016 Daniel Abdal-Hayy Moore
All rights reserved.

FIRST EDITION
ISBN: 978-0-578-17791-5 (paper)
Published by *The Ecstatic Exchange*,
6470 Morris Park Road, Philadelphia, PA 19151-2403

For quotes any longer than those for critical articles and reviews, contact:

The Ecstatic Exchange,
6470 Morris Park Road, Philadelphia, PA 19151-2403
email: abdalhayy@ecstaticxchange.com
website: www.ecstaticxchange.com

Cover art © by the author 2016
Back cover photograph © Author 2016

DEDICATION

To
Shaykh Muhammad ibn al-Habib
(and the continuation of the Habibiyya)
Shaykh Muhammad Raheem Bawa Muhaiyuddeen
all shuyukh of instruction and ma'arifa
Baji Tayyaba Khanum
of the unsounded depths

and my beloved wife Malika
and family and friends

•

*The earth is not bereft
of Light*

CONTENTS

Introduction by David Federman   10
The Match that Becomes a Conflagration   17
Fulsome Wind   18
In This World   19
How Can We Not Admire   20
Poem in the First Person   21
The Hawk Flies Past Midnight   24
Wine Poured Out   26
Not Mine   28
The World Went Away   29
Elephant Herd   33
The World   38
The Gorgeousness of the Shadow   41
The Boats   44
When the Circus Comes to Town   46
Sumptuous Sunken Pool   48
Tiny Scholars on Mountainpeaks   51
Green And Blue Marble-Sized Sphere   52
Enter Me into the Great Adventure   54
The Fish That Swallowed Jonah   58
Navigate That!   60
Such a Difference   62
First There Was Nothing   64
It Starts Out Small   66
Death Can't Get You   69
One Note Sounds   72
The Call That Takes Us There   73

Talking to God   75
Forever   77
Mouse Hole   79
If Your Vessel Springs a Leak   82
Of Course the Essence of it All   85
I Can't Prove God Exists   88
The Miraculous Scaffoldings   90
Took a Deep Breath   92
The Hourglass   94
Every Wind   96
The Bus of Bones   98
Multilingual Alabaster Candelabra   99
The Salient Thing About Sainthood   100
Sam the Big River   102
The Strike to Watch   105
Death Never Meets Us Halfway   108
While in This World   112
Saffron Edge and Lavender Center   114
No Second Face   116
The Magic in a Glance   120
When Seraphim Fly Overhead   122
The Most Beautiful Ship   124
A Pot of Ink   127
Sound Advice   131
Silks from Persia Gems from Yemen   133
Time Slides By   135
It's Not to Do   139
Dumbfounded   140
Bird Count   142

They Try to Approach   143
We Live in an Exquisite World   145
An Owl Flew Past   147
Are We Standing in One Place?   150
We're a Sensitive Bunch   152
If a Giant Ocean Liner   154
Music of the Spheres   156
Awakened by Nothing   157
Sharper and Sharper   160
Advice on Aging   162
Last Things   163
The Power of a Body of Water   167
You Take a Picture   169
Now We are a Norwegian   172
Coat Ten Sizes Too Large   174
Good Horse Good Horse   176
The Fortress Looked Down   178
Is It Too Late to Wonder   179
A Pin Drop   181
Everything Shines   187
Time to Wind This Down   189
No Two Alike of Anything   191
Try   194
Rough Country   196
Again and Again   198
I Enter the Chapel of My Forehead   201
Married to a Mass of Atoms   203
The Envelope that Contains the Message   206
A Drunk Juggler   208

How Many Chances   211
At Seapoint   213
Epitaphs   214
Finding the Right Metaphor   216
Love Boat   220
Golden Bucket   223
The Match that Became a Conflagration   224

INDEX   230

POETRY AS DEVOTIONAL PRACTICE

> ...the only real escape being
> a beyond that's within us
>
> that once within us becomes
> nowhere we can't
>
> call our own
> and our own we can
>
> only
> call His
>   — from *"We Live in an Exquisite World"*

Like so many artists of his generation, poet Daniel Abdal-Hayy Moore has origins as a writer and Sufi Muslim in Zen Buddhism, and it would be reductive to separate his poems from a lifetime of spiritual practice and meditation. Hence it is important in reading him to be guided by — or, at the very least, cognizant of — the fifty years he has spent cultivating mindfulness in daily five-times prayer and *dhikr* (remembrance of God), spiritual fruit of seeds planted in the mid 1960s with Zen Master Shunryu Suzuki in San Francisco. I personally couldn't sound the oceanic depths or accompany him to the gravity-defying heights of his poems if I hadn't realized the intimate, indissoluble link between his practices as a Muslim and as a writer. "The Buddha gaze" is, for Abdal-Hayy, a kindred "God's Eye" with which he sees Creation or endeavors to see it. Indeed, his entire poetry can be viewed as a diary of daily life anchored in remembrance of God.

Abdal-Hayy is "summoned" to his art as he is to his duties of prayer, so the receiving and writing down of poems can, and should, be seen as a daily recording of consciousness contoured by years of prostration and recitation — for the most part peaceful transcriptions of realization, states of being and trains of thought encountered in the constancy and commonplace of devotion. In this regard, Abdal-Hayy follows a long lineage of devotional poetry at least as far back as Kabir, Rumi, Yunnus Emre and St. John of the Cross. This "call"/"calling" is described in the poem, *"The Call That Takes Us There,"* from this book. This poem could be as much a record of daily devotions in a Zendo as well as Sufi Lodge, where much of life is spent in "sitting."

> In our repositioning ourselves vis-à-vis
> the little doorway ornate and almost
>
> invisible that is ours alone into the
> specific corridors towards the Lord's
>
> Throne Room
>
> The constant little adjustments of
> repositioning to get it just right for a
>
> smooth going-through into what for
> each of us is certainly The Promised Station

The goals and preoccupations of the "sitting life" are quite different from those of the "standing life" with which we are most persistently engaged. In poem after poem, the poet addresses, or identifies, himself as a point, or node, of awareness in a vastness. In the constant expanse of Abdal-Hayy's poems, one leads or longs for a different kind of life than the ones we plan for in the more narrowly focused. Everything that takes place is part of a processional consciousness common to every extant spiritual tradition.

This isn't to say that Abdal-Hayy has disappeared or metamorphosed permanently into some state of cosmic disafilliation with the "standing life." Bomb burst, volcanic eruption, storm staccato on tin roof; sounds of misery and pleas for mercy from it are overheard in the generally warm and sturdy hermitage of practice and poetry that he has constructed during decades of devotion. But they, too, are part of this "tapestry of designations" —

> No metaphor or metamorphosis
> too low for God to coin in this
>
> perishing continuously
> assembling and reassembling world
>
> each part reconstituted out of
> sheer heart-thought in
>
> head space

Compassion is a rule of every road he travels. Any other road accrues karma and debt and, ultimately, mutuality of misery. Nevertheless, you can't be as at home in the wilds of thought and imagination as Abdal-Hayy is without having been lost in what Jack Spicer called "the dark forest of words" and frightened out of one's wits and wit. "How do you talk to God when your / mouth's full of flies?" he asks in one poem and then recommends "shutting down bone by bone" as a cure for distemper. This, as the mystics say, is to "die before death," and it is a deep freeze into which the poet has often willingly entered.

> The fact that things go wrong is
> proof that all is well that
>
> things are energized enough to go
> off their rails from time to time
>
> That people we love die is proof this is
> not a dumb universe whirring its
>
> blind cogs but its Creator is
> implacable in His Wisdom to give
>
> life and take it to Him at His behest and not
> ours in the strong magnetism of His Love

There is a disciplined severity of acceptance in those last lines that has nothing to do with resignation to death but acceptance, even affirmation, of it. Abdal-Hayy knows of what he writes. Now, in his fifth year as a cancer patient, the poet sees death as intimately near as a companion and so remains calm and poised.

> Somehow the Next World gets
> closer with each breath
>
> So it's wise to invoke its Owner
> with every breath we take

This advice should not be mistaken for caution. Throughout this book, everything that is seen — provided it is seen calmly and clearly — is part of a "generosity." This generosity includes death. Such feelings are possible, I think, when one's identity is sourced not just in prayer or meditation, but in a life where all is practice. Louis Zukofsy wrote somewhere that "Practice makes perfect" is only the beginning and that thereafter "Perfect makes practice." In short, living itself becomes an art of devotion. Part of Abdal-Hayy's devotion is to poetry. And when this art is at its fullest, the mind of its creator shines with an inspired light, bathed in a godly glow. In *"When Seraphim Fly Overhead,"* Abdal-Hayy describes seasoned devotion and its sense of "witness" (read: *with-ness*) like this:

> The seas never stop to look around
> but just keep ongoing and going on
>
> a million miles in all directions
> teeming with life
>
> in the courts of king and queen whales
> who continue singing their
>
> nuptial songs
> praising the One Who made the
>
> initial statement
> that started it all

Here I return to my starting point — namely, that Abdal-Hayy's poetry, like his life, reveals one of devotional practice. He is anchored in interlocking commitments to prayer, meditation and writing, as well as a life as husband and father, son and participant in whatever God presents to him of this world or the next. This confluence has resulted in an extraordinarily articulate and steady mindfulness. And at a time when Islam is more and more associated in the media with a metastasis of nihilistic terrorism, and many are skeptical about its proponents' claims that it is a "religion of peace," let books such as *"The Match that Becomes a Conflagration"* serve as a convincing Exhibit A toward proof of that premise.

— David Federman, Ardmore, PA, February 22, 2016

The cave you fear to enter holds the treasure you seek.
— Joseph Campbell

Be beneficial wherever you go, and never cause any harm; be joyful and radiant, and do not become angry; leave disputation; never go anywhere without purpose; and never laugh without amazement.
— Hazrat Khidr's advice to Sayyedina Musa (Moses)
as recorded by Ibn Kathir in *Qisas al-Anbiya'*

My God, blind is the eye that does not see You watching over it, and vain is the handclasp of a servant who has not been given a share of Your love.
— ibn Ata'Illah

THE MATCH THAT BECOMES A CONFLAGRATION

A rash suggestion that such a
small thing might a mighty

conflagration make

one stick with a flagrant tip might
slip the knot that keeps the whole thing

tight and blast it into flame

Does this world have anything to keep?
Let me count the ways —

A dimpled face of flushed joy
hands capable of molding clay or

piano runs to outrun Rachmaninoff

Long nights with old wood wheels scraping the
road

My Beloved at the window signaling
sundown

Face turned away into a greater space
billowed with night clouds filled with

ecstatic fulsomeness

10/14

FULSOME WIND

Why would we want to stay long
in a place that causes such grief?

Why hold onto tent pegs even after the
tent's long gone?

Being born is the investment? Once here
rabbit-eared or human-hearted we

want to stick it out beyond the end?

A few lettuce nibbles or love-trysts enough to
extend our desire? The hovel

nearly falls over and each season
leaves turn gold then brown then

dead

until Spring
springs again into bloom

But each year we might sag a little more
and our sails not fill out quite so

full
in such a fulsome wind

10/14

IN THIS WORLD

In this world matter and its
sliding magical properties of

panels and sides shifting into and
out of place with some occasional

rests in between its constantly
hectic molecular activity

all created this way to keep us
busy perhaps at all hours

even asleep when the
shape-shifting increases in our

shut eyelid movie theater
and we also shifting into and

out of shape as implausibly
plausible as water flowing

every-which-way in
Godly focus

gone really in a flash almost
before it's begun

10/14

HOW CAN WE NOT ADMIRE

How can we not admire
emptiness especially when it's

pregnant with superlative Light?

Explosively thrilling in its opening of our
perceptions from toe-tips to galactic

distances more numerous than
sand grains in a colossal

stretch of beach

that turns inside-out instantaneously
this world and all its gala self-

advertisements

to an interior smoother than conch-shell's
mother of pearl and

more radiant than all of underwater
Neptune's kingdom of diamond thrones and

glittering tridents of purest porphyry!

10/15

POEM IN THE FIRST PERSON

Wait! Before you begin a new poem
do you really want to add yet one

more to the planet's population of unread poems?
Are you so sure what emerges will be

among the read ones the ones in their
own daylight aboveground leading

happy lives as part of the melodious family of
read or at least skimmed over or even

half-heartedly glanced at poems?

Those of us who are among the unread
have to hang out in neon-lit 24 hour diners or

hospital emergency rooms in case someone
somewhere might turn to us or happen upon us

and begin reading silently to themselves or
on a good night or day

even read us out loud
(I'm thrilled at the prospect!)

We all have to be on call and all our
ducks in a row so to speak in

readiness but you should know
we're the Silent Majority we poems

gorgeously written but
never read

I don't want to discourage you and
getting read may not be

uppermost in your mind as you set out yet again
through the beast-ridden savage forest of a

new poem

Maybe for you a poem being
alive anywhere under

moonlit clouds in a haunted purple
landscape with wide-eyed creatures is

enough and if someone should actually
turn on a light and read it and it flowers into full

Technicolor and sense-surround sound well
bravo!

And if it stays in a
dark drawer as so many of us did for so

long with Emily's tidy
ribboned bundles that's

Okay too —
Go ahead!

Write on!

God speed

and good luck!

                                                        10/17

THE HAWK FLIES PAST MIDNIGHT

In memoriam Qadir Bibi Hackett

The dead seal in their last moment
and leave us outside

looking on in wonder

A face once so animated
now in stop-frame

The body that carried the soul around
discarded

leaving these imprints
of ever-shy animation

with a Ferris wheel whirling in the
background or

sea waves

and a sky more filled with clouds
than ever the face could achieve

in animation

Her color had become stone-like
she of the north country

and the bluebird poem she
loved to recite might have been

why her mouth was still open
and her weeping husband said he still saw

the twinkle in her eyes

She was definitely Joan of Arc
a more radiant Ingrid Bergman of

spiritual conflagration
where dross is burnt away

to pure essence

and the hawk flies past midnight
into heaven

    10/18

WINE POURED OUT

> *Everything we see in the world*
> *is what is in our heart*
> — Chinese poem *(as heard on TV)*

Wine is poured out on the ground
and gazelles spring from it

into the air

followed by lions who eat them one by one
followed by thunderstorms that frighten the

kings of beasts into submission to
the King of heaven and earth at one

crack of electrical night from which a
million new gazelles pour forth onto

the plains below bouncing for all their
worth into the golden

delight of our inward eye where all this
life takes place as we

drink God's wine from the sweetest
grape and pour the rest in joy

out on the ground

and are ourselves subsumed in the

great circle whose only death is

the next loop forward into the
King's Throne Room with no

body to speak of neither
gazelle nor lion neither eating nor

being eaten but only
sheer delight of the

inward eye where

all this life takes place

10/20

NOT MINE

I wake up in the night
with no end in sight

There's a Labrador Retriever
somewhere retrieving

There's a thief in the night
somewhere thieving

There's an eye that's blinking and
unblinking like a motel sign

There's a heart that's thinking and
unthinking in an atmosphere benign

A cliff that's a lift and a
cliff that's best left behind

A land that's both bland and
grand at the same time

and nothing of any of this
is mine

10/26-27

THE WORLD WENT AWAY

1

The world went away on a hunting trip
and left us alone in the

long and short corridors and sudden
staircases ascending heavenly levels

A gray light entered around us with
whispering tread and a soft

electrical energy whose crackle was a
new language to our ears but whose

words seemed to emanate from our
hearts

There were no edges or slopes no
ledges or shale cliffs no

entrances or exits all simply
spacelessly spacious and

timelessly timeless in a
placeless place whose

air was our selves obliterated
and whose Presence was

Allah

2

What kind of rose speaks to us out of the
grave of our selves?

What eyes look into our eyes
in the new place?

What road are we on when
all roads are gone?

If the truth speaks through us would
birds scatter from the trees?

How do we refer to this or that when the
self is obliterated

or is there a this or that instead of simply
one This and for all else the

same rose multiply
multiplied?

The beauty of a horse assuages the pain of
separation

The glistening gait of a horse
dissolves separation

The ecstatic gallop of a horse through
light after light brings

unity and separation both
into this place at last

and no rose blooms that isn't
the golden rose of a nothingness

that brings us face to face with the
rose of His Face

unveiled

3

I awake from a deep sleep into a
deep sleep

I could be aboard a windy galleon
tilting dangerously in a

thunderous sea

but I'm in Philadelphia in the same
room I went to sleep in

The same glow of a lamp overhead
keeping vigil above me

and any angels who might be near

whose world is this world as well as
the Unseen

intersectioned by our visionary treks in
sleep or in waking states

opening doors and
entering rooms in which

the Prophet Muhammad God's
peace be upon him might be

sitting surrounded by his
Companions

in the same glow of a
lamp keeping vigil above them

and he might just look up as we
enter and his soft strong eyes

lock for a moment with ours and
burn everything away that isn't

Allah in that sweet
incendiary instant

ELEPHANT HERD

A harpsichord on a lonely beach
played by a penguin

A lone boat with tattered sails
going nowhere

full of shining seniors

A long hallway nearly pitch black
with a ballerina in silence

pirouetting slowly

A rainbow appearing gloriously over a
canyon and

no one to see it

A lion staring at a hairbrush for hours
wishing he could

run it through his mane

People in a park completely oblivious of a
circle of angels around the

central fountain

A planet turning at a slightly different
angle to the sun and the earth's

oceans reversing

A fluttering over the city from
window to window but

no birds in sight

A bridge swaying slightly in the wind
and all the people passing across it

suddenly happy

A rose that looks at another rose
and bursts into tears

from so much beauty

A bicycle that decides to go out on its own
down dark midnight streets

and returns before sunrise

A tear that begins its ride down a
cheek not sure if it's from

excess of joy or excess of sorrow

A young giraffe that can't quite reach the

lowest leaves but

cranes its neck and suddenly
stretches its mind

A river nearby that notices the giraffe and
claps its hands in applauding cascades

A dragonfly skimming over the river
startled by the applause

The noise of clapping water suddenly
born in the air where

before there was stillness

now happy to be alive then
dissolving away

All the speech of the world
born into the air where

before there was stillness

then dissolving away

words called up from their
shaded coverts then left to

orbit the earth's rotations in humming
eloquence

sunlight expanding its chest to
breathe in the first

air of morning

Wherever sunlight falls there's a
sweet recognition

and an instant of awe

When we see a face in such sunlight
our eyes' gleams

jubilate

God's in the fineness of the vapors of
nothingness

and we instinctively know it in our
fingertips and heartbeats

each outbreath an
acknowledgment of His

superior Presence His
Majestic reticence

in which everything flowers

An ant whose destination is always
instantaneous

A pause in our thoughts that
asks to be left alone

An aloneness that is in itself
the highest glory

Schubert played it on the piano and
everyone was struck dumb

The little door of this poem is
slowly closing

The elephant herd has heard of
fresh pastures and

moves softly on

                                                          10/30

THE WORLD

The world by day is not the same world
as by the middle of the night

Whispers of mist along the carpet
and silence like a solitary phoenix

sitting among tall bamboo on an
island in the sea preening its fiery self

surrounded by coral reefs that go
down a mile through bright blue water

where Neptune holds court among his
ancient mariners

and nothing breaks through but Light
from an indefinable source

that is God is all directions at once

whose celebration is the same silence
that proliferates as daily noise

in the rhinocerotic roars of daylight

2

The Laws of Physics can

explain everything

except the Laws of Physics

3

Visions of Hell wait in their tacky
scorched costumes just offstage

for a cool entrance at our lowest moments
trying out various ghoulish laughs

and choice satanic whisperings
in the midst of our most vivid

flowery luscious glades and
melodious splashing streams

4

The fact that things go wrong is
proof that all is well that

things are energized enough to go
off their rails from time to time

That people we love die is proof this is
not a dumb universe whirring its

blind cogs but its Creator is
implacable in His Wisdom to give

life and take it to Him at His behest and not
ours in the strong magnetism of His Love

That days are coming we know nothing of
and days have left us

whose colors can still be
seen in our eyes when suns

rise and set in their glorious
golden raiments

That Space is the Lord and Time is
Allah and They are One Presence

and we within their palatial precincts
imbibe the headiest wine to the

end of our days and beyond

with nothing imperfect left in
and nothing perfect left out

when Time and Space are
brought back to God's crystalline House

and we reside within it with Him alone
in its resounding heavenly walls

                                                        11/2-11/4

THE GORGEOUSNESS OF THE SHADOW

The gorgeousness of the shadow God casts over His
entire creation

from His Light
is comparable to the blindness of a blind man

in a room filled with ceiling high
mirrors and candled chandeliers of

infinite cut crystal radiating in all directions

or the hoof beats of golden horses over
grassy hills at dawn entering the

full blast of first light when their
shapes disappear and only the bright

xylophonic sound of their hoof beats can be
heard on the already resonating tympanies of our hearts

as the entire earth falls away in its
stern orbit into radii of borealis curtains shaken

repeatedly across mountain peaks and
moonlit ocean wave crescents winking below

Our apprehension is positively
ant-like before this even as

we know the delectable shatterings of
pure beauty when we

see it and our own bodies
shudder at it

The most heavenly buzz of a
new star being born in a

million light-year away galaxy can't even
come close to the scintillations of His

shadow nor of how its purity sinks into

everything we are and live among
each desert sand grain a

magnifying clock of it each waterfall drop a
microscope of more unfolding

universes of it from only one
breath of His into the very

oxygen we breathe

eye blink after eye blink of it
recreated in our being

each pore of our skin a
hallowed repository of the glare shadow

cast deep into us by
His Light

                                            11/5

THE BOATS

So the first boat set out and
immediately sank

The second boat flew sails on
tall masts and capsized

The third boat bore into the
water with its loud motor and

burst into flames

Finally a great battleship was
brought in and got itself

torpedoed in twenty minutes

A fleet of yachts fanned out
and each met a watery death

in sumptuous splendor

Meanwhile Pedro in his
fishing boat continued

pulling in his net full of
flopping fish and smoked his

sideways pipe in the
forenoon

put-putting home by
midnight with a

boat replete and a

heart so God-connected the
waters seemed to part to

let him pass

                                                      11/7

WHEN THE CIRCUS COMES TO TOWN

When the circus comes to town
the roustabouts in their Can't Bust 'Ems

clear the grounds of debris and weeds
in order to present Reality

where people fly through the air with the
greatest of ease and

wild beasts are tamed by a
man with a chair

more clowns tumble
out of a car than ever went in

spotlights play on the endless raftered and ribbed
ceilings of heaven among the

guy ropes and hanging trapezes
elephants big as houses in docile rounded

lines head to tail lope in great pulsing
circles

and glistening and glamorous beauties in spangles ride
caparisoned horses throwing

kisses to the crowd endlessly smiling
A happy piping music suffuses the air

and a blue mist pervades everything
like a supernatural smoke

The ring master in a strong
melodious voice focuses our

attention on one of the three rings
presented before us

in their natural succession where things
happen

and falling flyers are caught by the
ankles or wrists to safety

as nets below them shine their intricate
mesh in the clear mental light

And when it's over we go out by the
same opening we came in thorough

into a sublimely different world
where everything seems even more

real than it
was before

11/7

SUMPTUOUS SUNKEN POOL

The sumptuous sunken pool at the
bottom of the ocean

lined in dolphin tiles and starry porcelain slabs
filled with a purplish water

The vault of heaven inset in the
vault of heaven

higher and deeper and teeming with
flora and fauna appropriate to

thin oxygen and less gravity

The world within this world
as if great sheets of organic glass were

walls within walls and labyrinthine extensions
where stroll the most magnificent strollers

down flowery esplanades between
fiery and radiant buildings of a kind of

rippling vapor in whose circling mists

people who are most like ourselves move and
circulate in varied costumes of

various intensities and levels of
seriousness in black and charcoal hues as well as

rainbow waterfall tissue-thin lit-up cloths more
suitable to dream figures than to

mortals such as we as they say though
we are more immortal in soul than

mortal in body and go on in
splendor through pools in the

sea floor as if diving upward
and heavens set within the

vault of heaven as if diving downward
and worlds within worlds which is in

fact our true home within our
truest nature

and our being within our being
that knows the radiance within the

within of the truth

closer to music than to tragedy and
more redeemed than damned by

rhapsodic airs meandering and
migrating forward around us

to the goal of our origin and the
direction of our most

nearest jugular directionless now
eternally new

11/8

TINY SCHOLARS ON MOUNTAINPEAKS

Tiny scholars on mountainpeaks in
fissures of rock are keeping the

scrolls up to date with moonlight in their
hair and tears in their eyes

Their smocks are moss-ridden and their
cloaks are refuges for both

foxes and hares as lights in the
skies around them flash and are

black then black again and suddenly white so

every valley lights up momentarily with their
subvocal speech as their

pens dipped in cinders and gum write and
small birds

congregate at their feet

11/9

GREEN AND BLUE MARBLE-SIZED SPHERE

The curious green and blue marble-sized
cloud-covered sphere suspended in the

air in a vast and airless
hangar-like hall

off a particular street in
cosmic space

and the people interested in
what it is and their curious

drawings of what they imagine we must
look like

generally octopus-like and of
peculiar colors and

faces with such things as
noses and eyes and especially

mouths in what seem to us like
arbitrary places

though with nothing at all to
go on except themselves I suppose we

can't be too surprised

They hover around us wishing for some
close-up magnification but it's

beyond their otherwise highly
advanced technology so that even

nearsighted with whatever
sight they must have they don't see our

cozy and smoking civilizations nor our
little forays in airships off the sphere from

time to time to a few inches
out into the airless space

and they don't see all the
warm puppy love that goes on on it

nor the violent outbreaks from
time to time the despair for the

human race and the
absurd hope

11/10

ENTER ME INTO THE GREAT ADVENTURE

1

Enter me into the great adventure

Don't let the Tygers of Wrath
pounce at the inception but

lurk at the sidelines behind
banana leaves the size of continents

waving in a wind as great as an
eyelash blink that fans the

cosmic spaces

Each step a plunder of the invisible
each departure a leaving of treasure behind

for the inestimable treasure ahead
Pearl of Great Price

haunted already by what we've
never seen

carrying the shadow that will be
cast down at the

death of our minor being to the

allowance through its empty gateway of Your
Greater Light

O Thee to Whom we turn without
turning but Who by true turning we would

return to Thee

2

The train leaves off its passengers
and goes on by itself

The fire consumes a mountain village
and then consumes itself

The sky beams down above a lake
then gazes a long time at itself

Eagles hover for a while in air
then fly within themselves with giant

wing-flaps toward heavenly light
that shines only for itself

We stand up for a time then
lie down in ourselves without having left nor

not having left behind the list of our
duties to be fulfilled by everyone but

ourselves

The day pulls itself over itself and
reveals stars beaming by themselves

through space that is
itself

where nothing but itself exists
to contemplate itself

3

How honest can we be
when everything's melting instantly?

We contemplate our features in a glass
and it too melts away into the past

The river washes all its suds around our feet
whose every crescent of its ripples can't repeat

The sun bends down upon our bending forms
whose only beckoning comes from earthworms

The sky fills with incredulous white light
that convinces us that everything's all right

and it is in every cranny of our lives
where zebras leap and honeybees keep hives

where lions snooze with muzzles on their paws
and everything's fulfilled by its own laws

created by the Lawgiver Supreme
whose proof exists in a single eyebeam

cast on the melting world before it melts
and leaves behind the mystery of its wealth

where nothing else is at all by God
Whose nothing else was Him all along

revealed

4

He is He

and none other is He

but He

And He is

everything

11/14

THE FISH THAT SWALLOWED JONAH

The fish that swallowed Jonah
was a minnow

since by shirking the command of Allah
he shrank to the size of a flea

Our shaykha says *"Multiply yourself by zero"*
which means we could be swallowed by

anything and still come out whole

Even the earth can't swallow
a wali of Allah

Their divinely soaked bodies radiant throughout
intact here as there in every

circumstance imperishable as light
whose speed has been superseded by

the saints' instantaneousness
as in the story of Suleiman

Bilquis' throne suddenly tangible
in intangible space

with no change of expression
on the saint's moonlike face

nothing changed but the throne's illusory place

No metaphor of metamorphosis
too low for God to coin in this

perishing continuously

assembling and reassembling world
each part reconstituted out of

sheer heart-thought in

head space

even our bodies
afloat in it

in His All-Seeing oceanic
heart-embrace

11/16

NAVIGATE THAT!

I don't know if there's anything as
delicious as this is

The sun is a golden ball bobbing on a
black sea

In the little world within that widens as
great as the sky

a crystal city sits on the sleeve of a singer
passing below the window of our longing

for life without cessation even beyond the
slatted gate at the end

We see over the tops of all the walls
around us

Herds of antelope fill the green horizon

The moon sails on oblivious to our
cries

Backs of geese catch
rays of the setting sun and turn

silver

If an owl looks you in the eye
eye to eye you're probably

sitting in a tree

I've seen light before making
rings around everything but

this is ridiculous!

It's as if matter became annihilated back
into its own essence

that turns out to be a river with no
end or beginning

Navigate that!

11/20

SUCH A DIFFERENCE

There's such a difference between
light and dark

Even the fish in the sea
understand this one

Spear-tips of armies pouring down
medieval mountainsides and the

blinding glint off their chest armor marching in a
continuous river under a

stormy sky as if
bright silver were a bullet heading

towards you
and the light in the eyes of a

beloved in a room warmed by a
giant fireplace and her

flushed cheeks contrast with the
whites of her eyes by the

crackling flames as words are spoken

and the words themselves might also be
occasions for light against the black

background of the surrounding
mental environment as

love thoughts are exchanged

as a boat on a huge wave falls into a
trough of dark

and thoughts of safety in God's universe
disappear in a flash of mortality's

light when all is lost
and everything in your world from

light to dark and back to
light again alternates until the

decree in your case actually
comes to pass and its unearthly

light shines its splendors on you
as you rise saved out of the

bleak surrender of the cosmos'
embracing dark

11/22

FIRST THERE WAS NOTHING

First there was nothing
then there was something

or perhaps there was
never nothing or that this

that we think is
something is nothing

or that something and
nothing are the same

that "nothing can come of
nothing" as Shakespeare said or

that the King is in both states
greater than both

equally Creator of either
and that this we think of as

something floats on nothing
and that this something doesn't

go back to nothing so much as
go back to the King

Who is greater than both

This hand that writes these
sweet nothings is in itself

nothing though for
me at this moment that's

hard to believe

11/23

IT STARTS OUT SMALL

It starts out small and becomes
a Behemoth

a little dust devil that
topples a metropolis

a small chair made of cane
that becomes an able throne Room of

gilded tyrannical power
that soon

splinters into slivers

A drop whose ocean
engulfs all

and drowns the fishes

A cloud whose sky
enters our mental pictures to become

a wide skyline of thunderbolts and
sunrises

gold in every corner
bursting into flame

a universe of a
zillion viable galaxies

where equally breathing and
heartbeating beings live their

cycles and go to their graves
enlightened or darkened as God

wills to every
stretch of the imagination

next door or flung to the
farthest reaches

where silver beaches
stretch into yellow seas

and coral-like trees
branch into blue skies

and peace descends on
everyone and

everything at once
down to the smallest sparkling

animal or hairy insect
as angels lean their scatterings of

otherworldly light on whomever it is
willed to fall

here as everywhere

                                                            11/26

DEATH CAN'T GET YOU

Death can't get you if you
dwell inside a cone of light

or on the fastest palomino leap the
incessant hedges of fearless generosity

in broad daylight

or hold within you the way a
crater holds a lake

a pure mirror to reflect divine sunlight

who pours in drenches from a
dimensionless "above"

Death has all the bicycles in the great
bicycle chase

but turning to face it with
perfect poise might

bring them all to their knees or
flatten their tires letting all the air out of

Papa Pomposity and Mama Arrogance that duo
whose food of course is mainly fear

And fear of death in every language is
as universal as lips and eyes and a

quaking heart

If an elephant stampedes do we run right
into it or stand to the side hoping it'll

miss us? When a tide arches over the
town do we expect to get drenched as well as

Sidi Ahmad or Johannes down the road?

When death visits a household
(and the Prophet once said "Bring me someone whose

household has not been visited by death" and
there were no takers)

can we melt invisibly into the wall we're
standing in front of or

go unnoticed out a door into
fresh air and eternal sunlight?

The Kaaba in the heart goes past
death in a wink and sits on a

snowy field where the giant reunion of
all humanity takes place

If we constantly circumnambulate it
with its cool air and coiling pigeons above it

circling like a cosmological occurrence
day and night that

human murmur whispering like the
Ocean of God's love at its base

all fear
disappears

                                                             11/28

ONE NOTE SOUNDS

The living carry the dead
and the dead carry the living

That's what it says
in the engine of the moment

The tree carries the seed
and the seed carries the tree

The slosh of it
clangs at the sodden wall

The design carries the drop
and the drop carries the design

and a deer steps through brush
into open sky

No one comes to take away the earth

No life disappears before its time

If everything lasts forever

one note sounds

11/29

THE CALL THAT TAKES US THERE

In our repositioning ourselves vis-à-vis
the little doorway ornate and almost

invisible that is ours alone into the
specific corridors towards the Lord's

Throne Room

The constant little adjustments of
repositioning to get it just right for a

smooth going-through into what for
each of us is certainly The Promised Station

utter silence hooting and hollering in
celestial harmonies there

and whose echoes we hear through the
transparencies that are there just for

us to hear

that draw us ineluctably to leverage and
align our positions with hope and

prayer that we'll find ourselves
inside where

giraffes sing full-throated song and
waters ring kaleidoscopically

It's the call we hear in our
innermost ear

The call emitted from our
innermost heart

that takes us there

12/2

TALKING TO GOD

How do you talk to God when your
mouth's full of flies

and your eyes fiery hoops

your limbs tread water and your
lower trunk full of sympathetic but

hectic marsupials fighting for
prominence

There's no turning back and going
forward is dunes after dunes of

shifting landscapes of
people dictating their heartfelt

opinions onto the evaporate air
that sucks back into you so that

while you're a cosmos on legs your most
far-flung galaxies are sending weak

radio signals that they're
full of life and only a few hundred

light years out of reach

Yet God's proclaimed He's near and in fact
nearer than near

nearer than nearness itself
in which we are

nearly inside-out with His nearness
so that the world we

are and the world we're in is absolutely
one and its dazzlements of sheer

beauty our beauty if we only knew

so that talking to God may be
shutting up bone by

blessèd bone and letting our
circulating blood and unbated

breaths do all the godly and God Forsaken
talking after all

tongue by
molecular tongue

12/9

FOREVER

A sandcastle stood up and
proclaimed itself permanent

but passing sideways crabs all laughed and
clapped their claws as the

surf covered over them
as they burrowed deep down in the

sand and disappeared

Even the sky isn't forever though it
go on and on into truly extraspatial

territories where anything can
happen and no doubt

does in some far off galaxy where

someone might be burning toast or
dropping an egg on a newly polished

floor the
size of the lip of an earth-orchid and

just as velvety

Forever takes place in a wink right
before our eyes and before we

know it it's gone

But we needn't worry since another
forever is slotting up to take its place all

slick and ready to go

Of course in standard earth-time we may normally feel
impatience and annoyance at not seeing

the enormous tunnel of foreverness
indicating its entrance in the

twitch of a gnat or a sparrow
landing on a feeder peg to

peck at seed

or in my own heart among the
other herded sheep on a

sloped hill clovered in glistening green
under a dazzling sun

each glint of which between its origin and
certain extinction

lasts
forever

12/10

MOUSE HOLE

1

If number
weight measure and gravity

disappeared what
world would we be in?

A vague presentiment
rustles about me

If things left their abstract
natures altogether

if everything were stripped bare
and only a

glare light shone
and on my soul

and also I were similarly
stripped and left bare

and a wind blew
to take all

dross away
and the bones of it all

held firm?

2

Discovering God in the act of
discovering God

like coming across a doe curled around her
fawn in a

forest clearing

There's something about the way
dust accumulates on

top of everything there's something about the
way a sunbeam from its source so

far away slants through a window and
warms us arm or back cheek or

cat having found a spot near the
table where light and heat hit best

or waiting with full attention for that
discovery the way a cat with

complete dedication waits for
days at an assumed mouse hole on the

strength of a single squeak from the
other side

God's all-sided Light on
every side at once

                                    12/15

IF YOUR VESSEL SPRINGS A LEAK

If your vessel springs a leak can you
swallow the deep serenity of the

entire ocean in a few great gulps
enough to set your ship on dry land?

The sky also is full of seagulls flying
across the sun and some

gliding albatrosses by moonlight and
goose flocks on their annual migration

backgrounded by stars and galaxies
their wide wings barely moving and their

forward bodies gliding their
pure hearts home

One wide eye drinks in the entire sky
and lidded darkens it to its

natal night

and the shut eyes of death seal the
whole sky off forever

onto the other side where bright
festivals take place in choirs

silent to ourselves on this side
but whose celebrations ring throughout the

worlds in a wave of whispers each star
resonates into chimes

If the entire earth becomes too hard
can we sink through it

into Light? Nothing of substance has any
substance and nothing of forever

lasts forever except forever itself
and dust floats upward to its

source and whales eye us all
with God's smooth wisdom that

floats past and out of sight
taking its time as

dispassionate as time's entire ocean
wave after green wave rolling

over and over and
filling the world back

up again until we
begin where we

started and
swallow the whole ocean back again

into our hearts

12/17

OF COURSE THE ESSENCE OF IT ALL

Of course the essence of it all is love

How else explain the hardest blackest
coal nugget turns to diamond clenched

in earth's rockiest deeps?

How else explain a mother penguin
returning from miles away goes

right to her squeaking speaking offspring
somewhere in the middle of a few thousand

pretty identical penguins to our eyes and ears?

How else explain us all sitting here or
standing in a doorway idling our motors or

walking at a brisk or leisurely pace down a
crowded street at noon and

back to our comfortable chair or bed or
grave at last with God willing a

smile on our face?

The wave of it washes over all of us in its

tea-for-two billion tsunami its
sit-down-under-a-tree until enlightenment

earthquake its be-called-out-from-the-cave by
Gabriel standing on the horizon head

gone into clouds designation of
prophecy on Muhammad peace be

upon him with each gnat's wing beat here and
in all starry eternity forever?

Love seeps through our pores blasts through our
walls bounces along sound-waves careens

down deer-stampeding mountainsides
and up opposite slopes into cascading

sunlight

It bubbles out of our eyes and back
into them again with

what's in our hearts just as
everything we see outside is what's really

inside us in continuous animated
conversation one on one face to face

with God

So it has to be the essence of everything or else we'd
be swept away faster than a gambler

sweeping his winnings into his arms and
running out the door

or swifter than anything sliding off the
surface of a rotating onyx marble in

space as it hurtles towards it doom

Each breath a star orchard
each shine a rosebush of voices

jostling their fragrant petals each moment for a
higher-pitched purer sound

Each love twinkle or love rush
proof of itself alone forever

inside and outside of time
both profane and sublime

12/17

I CAN'T PROVE GOD EXISTS

I can't prove God exists
but I know I'm happiest when I think of God

blowing a rosebush into bloom
the way we blow up a balloon

or saving a bird from a drainpipe in the
nick of time though it was

me who opened up the pipe and it was
the sparrow who beat its wings

piteously for two days until I realized it
could be released and when the

duct tape was torn off and the pipe at last opened
after it fluttered a bit among the

dead leaves at the bottom elbow where it had fallen
it flew off into the trees and was gone

and I thought of God Who
kept the bird alive and hopeful and

inspired me to
make that extra effort to release it

And bridges over great bodies of dark water

and air ships lumbering through dark skies

It releases our hearts into outflung territories to
see God's endless majestic as well as

minute activities in this world shuffling their
veils and unmasking their mechanisms in

shuttering hinges and then
it's another world altogether God-drenched

God's gaze flowing through it all in perfect
waves like the engraved lines under a

magnifying glass of a William Blake engraving
each etch in perfect flow endlessly outward

that Godly frizzle along the vein of it
which by itself is a barren landscape

but with Truth's Presence springs to life

and His bent down and blown through
pure rainbow colors

irradiate it full

12/18

THE MIRACULOUS SCAFFOLDINGS

The miraculous scaffoldings that
keep it all going

The underneath drama behind a
usually bland façade

The multitude of angelic forces holding
this cell and guiding that molecule into place just so

not a millimeter off or else duck might be
moose and earthquake fiesta

Every drop that falls from the sky or
blade that pushes its great green

sword up from the dirt to
swagger in the sun

The panorama behind the panorama we see
whirring its invisible merry-go-round

so that I stand and go or she
steps out of a carriage to be

taken in to an audience with the Pope
in 1653 before marrying a Medici

and causing havoc in Tuscany

or butterfly in Brazil cantilevers a
whirlwind in the Sahara or

cloud across a city looks like
Armageddon in flames to all the

astonished onlookers below who
suddenly hug their children

and the angels with serious
expressions on their radiant faces are only

doing God's bidding according to their tasks
as everything fits with a

carpenter's precision joint to jowl
to the incessant Glory of His command

Who never
ceases

to astonish us

12/19

TOOK A DEEP BREATH

The night was perched all around with
hooting owls on branches in the dark

some flying with their enormous wings
in constant intercommunication

Green water curled up its lips at the
land's edge under a smudged moon

Owls' eyes could see it all
No mouse was safe

They ran along under
leaves as best they could

knowing full well they had owl eye
radar on top of them at all times

A snap crackle or pop and an owl's
head swivels in its direction

The mice were saying their prayers
under their mousy breaths

mouse hearts going like mad
moonlight seeming to

spotlight bright light between any

crack in the leaf cover

Lovers touched pink noses before heading out
spouses lightly brushed each other's paws

took a deep breath before scurrying

While whoever's the owls' predator
had its eye on the owls —

eagle or wild cat God's Eye honed to
razor sharp sight

the whole sky
the whole night

                                        12/23

THE HOURGLASS

The hourglass through which the
sand of our time on earth falls

on a table on a foundering ship at sea in a
lightning-storm that threatens to

overwhelm it

inside a glass bowl usually reserved for
gold fish on a table in a grand

drawing room of a castle in a
city under siege for three years

in a sandbox of war games on a
table in a floodlit room attended by

bored businessmen who unbeknownst to
them are in an angelic holding

state where each action lasts an
eternity and has the

meaning of a thousand saints each in their
own retreat caves in a holy hillside in

Turkey above the Aegean sea each
simultaneously holding in their

hearts a godly contemplation about
earthly versus celestial time and how

one is a blink and the other a river full of
stars that goes onward inwardly unwinding its

repertoire of symbolic events each one of
which is mirrored in our actions

made to emanate from our innermost
beings by divine decree in the

time it takes one sand grain of our
time on earth to fall through our

hourglass gleaming in God's
intimate sunlight

                                                  12/24

EVERY WIND

Every wind blows over
leaving some trees standing

some trees down

some walls left where they were
some wells still filled with

depthless water

Echoes dwell between words
reverberate back to pure originals

spoken by God in a divine wind
that came to Job and still

circulates

where night doesn't quite
reach down to the wall

nor filter
between the leaves of trees

to the bowed horizon
where we dwell

walking in our ancient garlands
in the circles left by the

ancients before us

though we step out naked from
time to time to let

His sunlight bathe us

He speaks
and the whole becomes an ear

to hear with

No distance too far
that He hasn't already reached

and the echo returns to us already
dressed in His Splendor

Even if you speak too loud
the spell can't be broken

and if you speak too softly
caterpillars hear beforehand

what they'll become

THE BUS OF BONES

The bus of bones stops for us
and takes us heavenward

by way of corpuscular slums and
the ups and downs of incorporeal mountains

hairpin curves and sudden stops to let
ghosts on or off and non-ghosts jostling for

their ever-vacant seats to sit by windows
smiling at all the swiftly passing landscapes

more luminous than dreams

1/3

MULTILINGUAL ALABASTER CANDELABRA

The multilingual alabaster candelabra
pouring down its

influences to beam us speak
different languages each vowel and

consonant verb and noun in perfect
placement germane to each tongue

Aleut to Nicaraguan Amazonian to
Wall Street shouted billionaire transaction

over scratchy telephone

soothing mother's lullaby by
Babylonian waters bubbling as they

burble by in communicable cadence

The Mercy of God in each spoken awareness
made pliable and heartfelt by

words in intuitive order none
wasted nor left unsaid in our

endless speechifying by the billions or over the
garden fence in sunflower sunlight

or whispered in a lover's ear
at moonlit midnight

THE SALIENT THING ABOUT SAINTHOOD

The salient thing about sainthood seems to be
the inconceivable becomes commonplace

plus a consistent sustaining energy or
light that carries even in the

quietest moments and the saint's insistence
it's nothing to do with them

and all to do with God Whose
Everpresence now

floods the room or hilltop where for a
moment the saint stands and the

whole world becomes evanescent while
he or she is the permanent thing

though they die
as it continues to circulate through

countless others
God's non-confinement

in any one thing

but all things at once
in His Oneness

So grass blades shout Hosanna in
silence when a saint passes over them

and standing on a small bridge
the waters below briefly

stand up to honor him or her as well as the
sky reflected within them

The key being a tranquility
so God's Munificence

falls through and sparkles
out in it completely

1/6

SAM THE BIG RIVER

Sam the big river
flows in a curlicue

Chan the lesser
flows in a near-perfect zigzag

Har the third river
crosses the two

The voice of the rivers
is always calling

None but the deaf
can stand on their banks

without smiling

Day and night
the names of all of us

are called out

Toucans fly between the
crisscrossed calling of names

Our names are called
not to confuse us

but to assure us
we exist with certainty

and purpose

That we were born
heading in a

single direction
through everything

and that God's Beneficence
dominates in every circumstance

The air crackles
with this resonance

We can't possibly get lost
with such affirmation

This tapestry of designations
makes up the world

His Presence envelopes
each designation

If we let go
it holds onto us

Wild birds weave all the
names in the air together

They're only reflecting
the names in the highest heavens

where in fact
the three rivers originate

each sparkle of light from their
surfaces casting

the light of our faces

from God's single original
Face in the Unseen

that has always been there
as if nothing else mattered

and nothing else does

1/7

THE STRIKE TO WATCH

The strike to watch is the one
that brings down

handwriting against the sky
or high singers upside-down

from the clouds

When roofs catch fire from its
lightning-quick electric illumination

Allah's intended something for us
serious to look at

and if some of His creation
fries his tears will be

mixed in with the debris
and a distant voice will

tell us to stand up and
take up the crossbeams to

rebuild and return having
counted the dead and the

living an always
constant in perfect balance with its

fluctuating sum

The silhouettes of horse teams against the
sky may bewilder us at this

late date but remember they've been
riding this way for centuries longer than

modern conveyances and the
sound of their hooves

soothes our hearts

What are these white lanes down the
ribs of the earth if not the

strike's path and emblem of His
visit to us one moment in time?

Have we heard the message of the
return of doves to the minaret

where they've brought up generations of
their own kind?

Have we heard the forlorn foghorn
where there's no ocean and the

only lighthouse for miles is the
one behind our eyes and hearts that

makes sense of all this?

We won't speculate how the
beach sand grew closer to the

foundations having to travel many
days and night to do so

nor the curious turtles
crossing the streets by moonlight

1/8

DEATH NEVER MEETS US HALFWAY

In memoriam Jamar Ferrell

Death never meets us halfway
though it cast a pall over our

happy roadway

It comes out of the festive party
in monk's robes

Grins through missing teeth
though it leave its tooth marks

when it will

Death at least would prefer a
raging ocean under a thundercloud

sky for backdrop than say a
24 hour burger joint with

florescent lighting though it will
do

especially if there's a
motorcycle stand out front

Death sometimes puts on a
silly hat or really expensive shoes

for fear going barefoot will expose its
peculiar toes

Death has peculiar toes
partly for the climb up the jagged cliff

overlooking that tumultuous ocean
where all hands went down

though it doesn't need a full moon
except on special occasions

a birthday or coronation

Death plays fair and square
in a disguise of unfair and wholly

round
in order to come round where and

when least expected to close the
definitive circle

Al-Ghazali said
"Live each moment as if

you'll live forever but
do the prayer as if you'll die tomorrow"

Sound advice in this
land of silence

There's never an ounce but that
a pound of it feels the same

There's never a pound of it but that
an ounce will do the trick

Animals will stop eating
to gaze intently at us in silence

at the majestic moment of it
with its backdrop of colossal

waterfalls whispering polyphonically
the sound of it transformed into

scintillating light
each droplet pounding the rocky base in

appreciation of our brave endurance

It's God's business completely
with no room for error

each measured to the perfect
micrometer

and taken with the least fuss

All the empty horses
suddenly have riders

All the empty waves
suddenly have canoes

All the empty skies
suddenly have angels

We can't know the intimacy that
comes with it

between the dying one
and God's breath

All the sounds have echoes

All the dimensions have gateways

All the extended spaces
have open arms of light

to catch us

1/10

WHILE IN THIS WORLD

While in this world
there's always something

A kangaroo mother gives birth in your
front yard

When you've got everything nailed down
the roof flies off

You invent a wheel-less bicycle and
one rides by with seven people on it

As soon as you've fixed your rotator cuff muscle
supraspinatus your wisdom teeth need pulling

It's the light and shadow play of God
tossing us on the high seas of His Love

Like those Innuit joy fests throwing folks
up in the air and catching them in a

blanket held by the whole village

though in this case what catches us
is also always something

a phone call from a childhood sweetheart
when you've locked yourself out of the house

a door that suddenly won't open
but you've just won the Sweepstakes

We're on a round earth with jagged edges
an oval ball in space with sudden

twists and turns

though like the endless gaze of God
it goes on and on

with everything in it
popping perfectly into place

one thing simultaneously
and one thing after another

                                                                             1/11

SAFFRON EDGE AND LAVENDER CENTER

A saffron edge and a lavender center
a sudden splash of bright yellow

as the sun comes up
a billion dot shower of darkness

as the sun goes down
melting into its own gold

a mellow liquid amber
running through it all

He puts his hat on and all color
becomes black and white

He takes it off and it's all
blues and purples then shot through with

bright full color again
in which we dwell

seeing yellow giraffe here
maroon rhinoceros there

striped tiger's wrath here
gray elephant's cool aplomb there

in this ever-exquisite paradise
shimmering before us

lining up in perfect symmetry
and the one inside us with

everything outlined in bright
silver

1/12

NO SECOND FACE

None of the many images of action and entity make the Actor multiple in any way

So whoever rises above every vanishing thing will be shown existence without duality

— Shaykh Muhammad ibn al-Habib

Push aside the sauce they say
and there's the pudding or

push aside the consequences and
there's the intention

Push aside the subterfuge and there's the
psychology that engineered the

masquerade intended to
put us off the trail so carefully

plotted

That behind all appearances lies a
single source in multifarious

manifestations if only our momentary
discernment might pick apart the

distracting details enough to find
true causes

But it isn't all analytical or
philosophical or even psychological

A dancer moves to the center of a

stage to perform meticulous contortions and
flights of purest grace and harmony

hours or even years having perfected each
beat between each click of action

frozen in time as well as each
before and each continuous after

the dance master counting them out at the
side in scruffy clothes and the

dancer starting and stopping before a
room-wide mirror

And behind the dance-master's meticulous
directions lie ages of expertise

that know of no imperfection

And behind each slide and
sparkle of things or each

collision and resolution domestic or
international are ticks and increments of

perfectly faceted jewel-like eternities
seamlessly bound together between

the flow of befores and afters

a kind of continuous hum almost
audible in our hearts' ears

a kind of bobbing in the same waters by
moonlight or daylight

never a dull moment as each wave
ripples or crashes by on the

same sea
hiding precarious and mysterious

depths

And there is Allah in all this —
each Name divinely aglow as if on a

visible clock face whose energies
almost speak themselves in the

midst of confusion that's really a
profusion of clear articulation

made by the Single Source
from His ever

cosmos-wide
mirroringly

and singularly
placid place

                                    1/20

THE MAGIC IN A GLANCE

The magic in a glance or the
mystical rose on the lips

arisings and fallings through a
telescopic air

flutterings of nothingness
contradictions that indicate

God's Presence in a match flare
illuminations by starlight

A lunar landscape in the soul
a buying spree of the heart's

fearless generosity
leaping over fences of matter

into snow fields of sunlight

We can't contain it all
in its splendid slipperiness

as it slips out of our fingers
back to its original elements

and back again in Technicolor mirrors
where no one's reflection shows

But moose faces in
armchairs'

Flights of geese by their
inner compass

Fields suddenly extended all around us

The harvest's in —
tall shafts of wheat

a gold glow in God's moonlight

sharp as a pin
all around us

1/21

WHEN SERAPHIM FLY OVERHEAD

When seraphim fly overhead
do they dip their wings?

Is a gigantic falls like Victoria or Niagara
a hangout for swimmer djinn?

Sheer cliffs are nothing for
saints who can stride from

mountain to mountain in a few steps
passing whole cities in a

single stride and mountain peaks
in two

Is this universe we see with our
wee eyes anything like the way the

universe is? And can we

turn these wee eyes around inside to
really see?

There's a cypress tree like a green flame
flickering the sky

There's a hillside in a graveyard and all the
inhabitants are having a conversation

and *not* about the weather

There are dots and dashes everywhere
as we slowly decode the DNA that leads us

back to the initial statement that
started it all

Can we be surprised at anything?

The seas never stop to look around
but just keep ongoing and going on

a million miles in all directions
teeming with life

in the courts of king and queen whales
who continue singing their

nuptial songs
praising the One Who made the

initial statement
that started it all

1/26

THE MOST BEAUTIFUL SHIP

The most beautiful ship you've ever
seen in this world or the

next

of nothing but graceful curves and
curlicue lines flowing into each

other like the rolling waves under it

Sails spread to heaven on masts of light
more like flames of inner illumination than

canvas more like tissue of the vellum
pages of old books of Holy Writ

OK more like the wind itself that blows them
ever forward across open seas into

opening skies like diaphanous latticework

A ship with every surface polished smooth
no hard angles no impossible

curves except they're resolved in
superlative harmony

It moves through the water not like
thought in its jagged hypotenuse of

distractions or shredded geometrical squares not
this and that broken into clipped patchwork

but like thought surpassed and propelled by
heart's true destination from the start

flowing forward as a plow of gold
parting Spring's easy earth in its tillage

but sky become ocean and the great
seas become cloudless heavens of

blue more crystalline than the eyes of seraphim
our cherished boat in all its

intricate rigging now blending into the air
arching upward into

sheer nothingness
disappearing into the same

light from which it burst
prow-first into

God's intangible precincts
all its creakings become

high voices calling out to us to
hear and obey our first encompassed and

charted
direction

home

1/27

A POT OF INK

A pot of ink by a black river —
into which should I dip my pen?

See the cosmos in a loaf of bread
or loaves of bread in the stars?

The great eyes of vanished bison
glower at us across vast empty plains

The hoots of vanished Indian tribes
echo in the air

With our faces in the Unseen as well as
the Seen world how shall we describe

wonder? Or is
wonder even circumscribable?

Pharaoh's boat was found
buried in the sands of Egypt

far from any water
since it was only meant to

navigate a non-elemental Beyond
into which he would

slip like a hand into a glove
with all his people's noisy fifes blaring and

the barking of little red dogs

Somehow the Next World gets
closer with each breath

So it's wise to invoke its Owner
with every breath we take

in anticipation of His Generosity
pouring in our direction through every

nook and cranny
as we edge ever nearer

What's that herd of giraffes
loping in the distance?

How is it suddenly all the birds
have become so articulate

talking of their flights and where
the best seeds are?

Our foreheads have touched The Marvelous
and we still don't know it

Our eyes have seen The Glory
and when they blink they

think it's gone

If God is Manifest as well as Unmanifest
what is this I'm looking at?

A dark girdle has just been
sloughed off

A gleam of light has
burst through a broken window

An off-key trumpet
heralds the coming storm

The Pharaoh thinks he can
outrun thunder's fury

His boat is on permanent display
in a glass case in Egypt

near the Great Pyramid of Giza

No one's going anywhere
without God's permission

Show the ticket stub of your heart
every chance you get

The door's never shut
though we stumble toward it

I've lived to tell the tale
and it's not even over

It will tell itself
when it is —

Ink from the ocean
ink from the pot

Light from Allah
is all we've got

1/30

SOUND ADVICE

Perhaps it's best to act as if
the world doesn't exist

Can we be sure it does?

Or is it just an imaginary nightmare?

I'd rather imagine galloping horses of
all different colors endlessly

rainbowing down green hillsides

than bomb-blasted shells of cities and their
stretched-out citizens

and if we all did down to the last
man or child woman or Ancient of Days

maybe the dark miasma would burst
and we'd be in a sweet glade of bright

light at endless last instead of
endless strife

though the world go on without us
slamming into the same brick wall

and its people suffer unimaginable pain

with our hearts' hands held out to them
but our faces turned moonlike into

God's sunlight

1/31

SILKS FROM PERSIA GEMS FROM YEMEN

Silks from Persia have a high fascination
gems from Yemen fetch a high price

The eye's heightened light for such things
is no match for the heart's

translucence whose outpricing outstrips

everything outward for the inward
treasure whose password is not

Open Sesame but a series of
arches and bridges over

treacherous waters achieved with
God's anti-gravitational Compassion

Mercifully dispensed
that lifts us from this

morass at last onto a
surer footing where no

feet are needed though the road
ascend sometimes abruptly

depending on our predisposition for
such things and every

variation of tough

travel conditions and horrendous
weathers

This is all imaginal
for though I've put my

feet down hard I've hardly progressed
among the rocks and slithery

salamanders whose forked tongues
do wag

though winds do blow and bring no
news that's good

But there again all winds are
earthly and if we turn even a

portion of our backs to them
we face what few eyes have

actually captured on the
unseen screen ahead

TIME SLIDES BY

Time slides by with its
hands inside the gloves of a ghost

Whoever sees it come in sees it go out
but the shadows it casts

behind each fairly solid object in the room
against each fairly solid wall behind it

or each fairly solid something somehow
may be the most substantial thing about it

under linden trees along the river's shore
or equally horizontal with our forms in

snooze position

Time is death in designer wardrobe
with leaping gazelles all around it

and baby elephants practicing
lifting and lowering their fancy new trunks

Hug it as we will
it slips through us impatient to return

to its Mother Ocean
Timelessness

All in all
it might just be better if we

dove into its Mother Ocean in the
first place rather than

run along its banks hoping to
speed past or at least catch

up to it
as it slips into the sky's icy clouds

She looks through her fingers at us
and giggles so prettily we

forget we're standing on a cliff

Or he engages us in such deep
conversation about Orpheus and

his dolphins that we don't see the
curtains either being put over the

furniture or sliding off the silver rods that
hold them to fall into soft

fold after sand-like fold of
diaphanous cloth

at our feet

For some
time is a racetrack having placed bets on a

sure thing in the blur of the horses never quite
reaching the finish line until too late

For others it's in the racing saddle itself of one of the
horses with the most outlandish name such as

Golden Eternity or *Live in the Moment* or
The Snickering Bridegroom or

Death to the Imposter

But even though the winning horse we're riding
walks into the victory circle with

a bright flower horseshoe wreath around its neck
the green pastures and rolling hillsides of retired

race horses call to it or worse
the glue factory on the other side of a dark

highway where reeking mucilage is brewing

If time were something we could smoke
we'd smoke it

and it is

If time were flights of noisy geese going
south in beautiful patterns against a

pewter sky we'd see and hear it
and we do

If time were the embrace that
thrills us to our bones and into their

marrows where the sponge absorbs it
with delicious amorousness we'd

swoon around its sweet breath
and our eyes blinked open or

sealed shut would see it in all its
radiant glory assembling and

disassembling each starry galaxy and
dust mote before and within us

And it's in the sigh of relief when it
passes beyond us in a gurgle of new life

trying out fingers and legs kicking in the
endless midair

we're forever born into

2/5

IT'S NOT TO DO

It's not to do with a head full of facts
but a sensibility open to the

whispers of God in the midst of experience

however many curtains there may be between
us and The Throne

each with its own particular wind blowing

however many steps to climb to a
top that is always near even while

just out of reach

all our failings in a tight ball like
aluminum foil clenched to

throw over that fence where it
just might catch reflections from the sun

— that fence between us and

ourselves

DUMBFOUNDED

Dumbfounded
the dwarf of insight took a route

different from ourselves and
got there before we did

Our senses in their conglomerate
opened wide to

see what they could see

Mysterious movements were
coded messages meant to be read

but deciphered at leisure under a
bronze boat

The sun's rest mode
of which there is none or else

we'd all go dark and our own
pocket of the universe

sewn shut

I love our listing of
worm holes black holes bends in space

from our comfortable position
this side of Venus

but some discomfort may be
the best state to be in

after all

2/6

BIRD COUNT

What was so touching about the
big flock of sparrows that

flew onto the telephone wires while I was
stopped at a red light

was that after the main group got
settled another smaller bunch of

ten or twelve flew on landing at
one end and then another smaller

group of four or five seemed to come suddenly
visible out of the sky itself onto a second

wire at the opposite end

and they all stayed put
arrayed along the two wires like

black commas as I
tried to count them

before the light turned green
against the great gray sky

THEY TRY TO APPROACH

They try to approach with explosives
but the Throne of Allah stays

implacably still
radiating its concern

The silence of the sky is not His
lack of articulation

but one of the salient features
of His Speech

If a window goes up and
someone leans out

where before there was no one
does that mean that until then the

building was empty?

I want a river of jubilation
and the camel driver's

endless song

Storming heaven was
never a good idea

A mother suckling her young
knows the truth of its intimate

location
be it human woman or doe

on her nest of pine needles on a
forest floor

They try to rattle the windows when
no one's there with

hand grenades

But He Who Sees it all in one glance
has already nodded His approval or

displeasure before the
dust settles

and the pain that rips through the
human body

is the harsh song of God's rebuke

Come

Approach it as you would
a stern superior

and watch love's waters
flood toward you

WE LIVE IN AN EXQUISITE WORLD

We live in an exquisite world
whose imprisoning bars are so far apart

you can barely see them

but only golden mountainsides of
trees reaching sky

skylarks ascending and
falling in song

and the best love people can muster
under the circumstances

and the circumstances are brutal

a darkness at either end of our lives
and the laughter of matter

From time to time a radiant being walks through
and the light cast gives all things voice

and all things cry in a most piteous way
to be released into the golden cast of the

light being cast by him or her
and our hearts leap in their cages

and our bodies' doors creak open a little
to see with eyes not our own

what can stand without shadow
both inside and outside us

At these times sky with all its stars
is exchanged for a Beneficent Face

leaning to smile
and all space filled with His Light

almost indistinguishable
but the Radiant One never stops

pointing skyward to accentuate
the difference

the only real escape being
a beyond that's within us

that once within us becomes
nowhere we can't

call our own
and our own we can

only
call His

2/17

AN OWL FLEW PAST

An owl flew past who
saw the miracle and remained calm

A river rushed past who saw it
and deliriously gurgled

Stones saw the miracle scattered wherever they
were and still had that stoned look

The miracle pervasive as air itself
from the pulmonary larynx a song with

each breath

to the Atlas mountaintops where
snow melts in four part harmony enough to

make you swoon

I witness it now in the chill of Fez
the shadow I cast by lamplight

onto the floor
and the whirr of the hotel heater

trying to keep warm

The manifestations of God's actions in the
world are not hard to see

maybe you have to have God's eyes to
see them

by which I mean love's lenses in
our own ant eyes enough to see

what's here in that place neither
completely inner nor completely outer

through whose telescope's wrong end we see
the world as big as we can

great earth clouds over the sun and the billion
galaxies light years away whose

mysterious motions show happy magnetic
populations at play

but through heart's eyes and heart's ears
where air itself a conductor of

light is a full orchestra of the
miracle and right now I hear the

wind section softly sighing
and sometimes the tympanist can't help

playing every other beat along the
street and the violin section truly

serenades us in the rustling of leaves
and the eyes and ears and general

sensorium God's given us are the
direct witnesses themselves to God's

miracles upon us
not even needing the gallop of rainbows

over the next hill toward us right now
to convince us

2/18

ARE WE STANDING IN ONE PLACE?

Are we standing in one place?
Do we move at all?

Tumultuous avalanche and
erratic behavior and

where are we?

A wind blows and we're
off again

But are we?

I stand in one place and
wonder

where the movement is
and if it truly moves

or if the world around us
is the changing thing

New pictures on the walls
new walls in the air

between one room and the
next

or are they?

I saw a toucan fly across the
road in Nigeria into the

jungle trees

Does that count?

Are we anymore transformed from our
ten year old self?

Has the transformation into Light
been complete?

2/23

WE'RE A SENSITIVE BUNCH

We're a sensitive bunch

Not like those tube worms by those
heat vents undersea

who seem to thrive on being boiled

We're soft centered and so
utterly vulnerable more like the

undersides of turtles when
flipped on their backs

Any slight makes our tentacles quiver
our very pink innermost parts cringe

A wind blows and we hunker down
a hurricane blows and we're

carried away

We get so easily carried away

Theologians ponder how many angels
fit on the head of a pin

but I ponder how many
billions of sensitive souls on this

rapidly whirling space orb fit
thick or thin

guarding our eyes against prying and
blasphemy while hoping for a

peek

listening into the barren canyons of our hearts
for words of solace and support that

keep us smiling inside and
glorifying the Source of our

tremulous serenity

3/1

IF A GIANT OCEAN LINER

If a giant ocean liner crashed through the wall and
splashed down next to you the

size of a tiny boat in a bathtub would you
be surprised?

Of course you would

If a clown came at you and suddenly became a
thousand clowns glittering in the sky and

slowly revolving like the constellation say of
Cassiopeia could your astonishment

be any greater? *I really*

doubt it

If our city streets started getting
wound up on a spool like so much

satin ribbon wouldn't we begin to
have little confidence in our so-called

hold on reality that somehow negates both
flying horses and their prophet riders as well as

the existence bisecting this world of
other more vivid and existent worlds than

this one whose double entranceway is the
heart within each of us whose door is

sublime recognition of the Divine Presence and active
invocation and repetition of all His

Names and Attributes whose constant
roulette keeps all worlds both

seen and unseen going?

A tranquil astonishment
a serene ecstatic comprehension

as all things stay on track as well as
fly off them like sparks train wheels make

trying to brake

each spark a world in itself
held to its source by the

sound of His Name intoned

3/2

MUSIC OF THE SPHERES

The music of the spheres
is lodged inside our ears

3/5

AWAKENED BY NOTHING

To be awakened by nothing
brought back into the expanding

space of the room you fell asleep in
now the "dead of night" as they

say though not dead yet by a
long shot

blinking eyes open and
turning on the light to be greeted by

the same or seemingly the same
four walls you fell asleep in with the

same pictures in their frames
the same geegaws hanging from the

ceiling the same air purifier
whirring in the corner thanks to the

happy continuity of electricity plugged in
awake or asleep the sparkling

charge running the machine the same as
that spirit electricity running us even when we're

unconscious and in no way

managing anything in any effective manner

that pure something-else having
taken over He Who sustains us

awake or asleep effectively maintaining
His decision concerning our

status vis-à-vis life or death
awakening us into

this world or the next at only
His behest not our decision

whatsoever
each breath a

millennium in full swing
a population explosion and

demise
an entire fanning out and

folding in again of a life
an existence of

gnat-like proportions
running on His wheels and

none of our own
at His rate of speed through

His doors opening like clouds or
narrowing into daily

corridors with
airplanes droning overhead

and our souls like silent armless
symphony conductors with the

music going through us all
around us simultaneously and

totally

no obvious source in sight
or sound

except this indefinable high-pitched hum
of everything at once

sun and moon and
all the stars

SHARPER AND SHARPER

Sharper and sharper the fine point hones
in on the unsayable that can't stop talking

which seems to be the way of it as the
actual living creatures of words begin to

circle it docile but determined like a
corral of beady-eyed language around an

invisible and inaudible center as if
seen from above

on this round planet in flat patches of
effective living space held in

space and to the planet itself by some kind of
animal magnetism faithful to the core

each of us individually similar in
geometric and physical composition

each of us a secret within a secret in the
heart unsayable and in a giant

cloister of silence surrounded by solemn
cypress trees filled with fantastical

multicolored birds creating an intricate
sound tapestry of air interwoven in all

constancy with The Divine Name

everything intones as always aforementioned
in these pages and on every page ever

worded and wreathed with any
simulacrum of meaning

closer and closer to the sweet bone of it
the beating heart of it independent of us

but of crucial centrality to us atom by
atom and person by person

identically so in incredible synchronicity

amen

3/9

ADVICE ON AGING

Do it when you think of it

Don't wait until after

to forget all about it —

Or don't do it when you

think of it

and forget about it

3/14

LAST THINGS

For Tamam and Shabda Kahn

1

The last rhinoceros might look around and
wonder where its beautiful beady-eyed

brothers and sisters went

The last waterfall might slide its
last cascade down the usual

rocks and feel strange

The last wheeling bird so used to
wheeling within other wheeling birds'

orbits against wandering clouds —

The last wandering cloud might wonder why
only one shadow is crossing the

earth below

Last things amounting to all the things that ever
went before

last movements shuddering into a

final stillness and a

final stillness hovering in its solitude a
moment before shivering away

We wonder whose eyes are
looking into ours for the last time

whose voice not heard up close but
neither too far away echoing faintly

whose face we gaze into before it
sets like the last sun with all its

energy drained

And then the Prophet's light and its
prophetic treasury whose

ocean-beats billow behind all vanishing things

and the ache of a planet out in
space at a dark edge with endlessness

alone among last things

when even all creation was a cure
for God's lordly loneliness

— and the last flickering gnat aloft in a beam of light

and the beam of light itself
lost in the Lord's bright Eye

2

Will we take everything by the hand and
help it through the last door?

When we boarded the plane the smiling
purser asked if San Francisco was our

final destination
of course I couldn't help myself and said

"I hope not —
God is"

And he strangely said
"I'm already there!"

Maybe he's too busy to ask him what he
meant

rushing back and forth down the narrow
aisle bringing tea

or maybe so much flying through the air
has finally gotten him there —

We churn through the night going through
last door after last door in space

each person of us on this plane a
world abuzz with its curious proclamations

and my sense of lastness always so acute
this far off the ground

through door after door in the
darkness

Each of them God's door
open for the first time

then vanishing away

                                                          3/14

THE POWER OF A BODY OF WATER

The power of a body of water when it's still
is its reflectability

It sees all the stars however far away
and every bird that flies across it

The power of water in motion can turn a
turbine bigger than a house and

erase a coastal city off its foundations in
seconds and send everyone in it

to its depths

The power of the sky when it's still is its
covering us with serenity and clouds that

hover between us and terrific distances

The power of the sky in motion
lifts roofs and crushes iron complexes with its

multiple electric fists and balls of lightning

The heart enraged enrages the world
the heart at peace ripples out the

sweet nothingness of its resistance to

meaningless action

and glows green and gold concentric circles
to the ends of space

YOU TAKE A PICTURE

You take a picture from where you stand

In front of penguins
you take penguins

In front of canyons
you take canyons

Carcrash Titanic tyrannical
downfall catastrophe

You take the instantaneous in
all its details all that

fits in the frame and implies by its
absence what's left out at the

sides top and bottom

or a moment later a year later a
millennium down the road when it's

all vanished entirely away
or has it?

Yet behind the picture is the
invisible presence the ocular

prescience that snapped the shot
then walked away

An absence whose presence is defined
by what's in the frame and if the

frame disappears do we get all the
penguins on that iceberg or every

crevasse in that canyon or does it

all just disappear with the
sound and fury of peace and disaster

equally silenced?

And if at the moment of
snapping the shot we disappear and

are no longer the choosing framer in
all our personal interference

does the picture get taken or do
clouds roll by and trees grow and

mushrooms sprout in God's glorious air?

Is anyone here?

Sunlight in the window hits the
yellow bromeliad that shines

and this room full of things
is still

And everything vibrates with Divine Names
under this hill

                                                           3/21

NOW WE ARE A NORWEGIAN

Now we are a Norwegian with
glittering red hair

Now we're the glisten on a swan's back
at noon

Now we're all rotations going
forwards and backwards and

towards the middle

Now we're a small planet in a trapezoidal galaxy
with electricity you can

take out of the air by a
snap of all your forty greenish fingers pointing

simultaneously

Now we are a peaceful and placid moment in the
middle of the ocean

Now we're all the sea's sea-creatures at once
awake and alive and hungry

The earth goes into its light and
dark phases and we're every

one of them both radiant and dull

Babies of all colors emerge from their mothers
by lamplight candlelight

fluorescent light daylight
and each one has our name

already sizzling in their hearts

And now is suddenly all there is for
each of them at full throttle

The eternal present expanding in
all directions at once for each of them

And now we're a pin dropping slowly
through space as if through glycerin

and now an incremental movement of icebergs in the
blue light of the artic

And now we're the whimper of an
abandoned baby wildebeest on the veldt

as well as the silent predator closing in on it
and the nightfall that

covers them both
with its starry

velvets

COAT TEN SIZES TOO LARGE

Where's the wisdom that wears a coat
ten sizes too large for it

or ten sizes too small so that
by nuclear pressure the light of it

expands into all of us?

Ten sizes too large so its radiance hangs in
floating curvaceous sheets over

deserts and mountaintops and each silvery cloud that
meanders into it is a grammatically

perfect sentence

Where's the wisdom that comes out from the
cups on the shelf and pours

itself into each liquid we drink
to pulse through our blood?

Owls fly through it as it hangs in
forest gauzes in the night

Moons show through it as its
fine stretched webs give it

geometrical perfection
with each symmetrical thread

Where's the wisdom that lands so
silently and looks around and holds out its

arms to fly straight into us as we
walk nonchalantly along and suddenly are

buoyed beyond ourselves into scintillant statures?
It's a glance off the ocean at a

certain time of day say around dawn
twinkling its crescent-shaped lights

or it's a whistling farmer in Bali
cultivating his terraced rice paddy

with lumbering sweet water buffalo
pulling him along

lanes of resplendent gold
into uttermost whiteness

3/27

GOOD HORSE GOOD HORSE

"Good horse! Good horse!" when I'm
patting the air and a

low bannister

Liftoff in the mind
over the rooftops

and since it's wingéd
a flapping of wings

"Steady now steady" as it
reaches the altitudes

overlooking the Pleiades
overlooking the holdup of the sky

its ownership from under me
ownership of heaven and earth

and all between

horse in outline in air
air in outline in space

space in outline
in endlessness

horse of it all
aloft

                                        3/28

THE FORTRESS LOOKED DOWN

*"The fortress looked down on the
burning plain*

*where rabbits in trench coats walked around
complaining of the*

bitter rain"

though no one for miles took
any notice of any of it

An epic moment lost in a
bubble of time

Still
I was summoned to write those

first lines down
and wait for further news

IS IT TOO LATE TO WONDER

Is it too late to wonder if I
hadn't been where I was would it have been

wiser to be where I wasn't?

Or that the city backdrop interchangeable with a
nice imagined seascape of wave-crests and gulls

would do best as psychic furniture
with some scattered sunlight on top

rather than these four walls not in
Singapore or Bangalore but

Philadelphia 2012 head somewhere in the
clouds as usual with watery eyes and only a

minimally leaking heart-valve according to
daylight's most recent cardiologist

We're all gathered together around a
small blue flame

If we blow too hard it'll go out
but if we breathe in some kind of

choir-like unison it may persist past even the
wintriest chill

Masked figures with antlers keep appearing
but they don't hang around too long

and leave enigmatic proclamations in
the air

like little thatch windows to look through and
little bamboo doorways to go through if we

make ourselves light enough and
small enough to fit through

And on the other side
rolling green extensions all the way

up into heaven
and in our hearts

rolling green heavens leading
down again to our walkable

real passageways while still alive
in exactly each place exactly right for us

and each place exactly right

3/31

A PIN DROP

1

A drawing slid under the door
a faucet left on and dripping

A helicopter out the window
no other messages for hours

A sound on the stairway going up
a grating fire escape chime

A siren from across town
a stillness unlike other stillnesses

Impossible to yawn or sneeze
a laundry list a hairpin

A slice of moon out the window
someone playing *Liebenstraum*

A long time goes by without notice
a cold chill runs up the spine

Down on the street a cough
the start of a soft tapping sound

A sense we've been here before
a sense this has all been made up

Time stopped hours ago
the room changes shape incessantly

A space where nothing's ever happened
a fine hair drawn between teeth

Don't dare move or it all comes
crashing

It's all come to this
tight as a fist

Nothing out the window but silence
a motor starts up and

drives off

Oh to be in that whatever
driving away

Nothing seems to matter
you are where you are

You can't turn on a light
but it's not getting any darker

You can see suddenly for miles
that gas station in Toledo

The waterfall in Maine
faces imprisoned in the past

Has it all been trying to tell you something?
Is it just now coming into focus?

It's been a long stretch of
not making sense

A silence unlike other silences
slowly coalescing

Why don't the windows fly off
How many stars can possibly

fit up there?

Why can't we speed among them?
We are where we are

exactly

A pin drops
and we're here

2

I don't look at all things
with a great invitation to die

That would be counter-productive
the room changes shape incessantly

If nothing makes sense wait till it does
if it still doesn't wait till it

doesn't

Every door doesn't open at once
not every door is closed as tight as

this one

Where the wall goes
so will you

Horses run free
because they're horses

The night sky is everywhere at once
the light in it is intangible

No one ever dies on purpose
even after the intention's been made

What happens at that moment's a secret
between us and all time and space

Its lips come right up to our ear
its eyes look right into us

It's closer to used than anything's ever
been before

Nothing between us and it anymore
The horses' flanks of it

shudder in darkness

The whirring sound of it
and the sizzle

Job couldn't resist its insistence
it insists itself in slow motion

We can't leave here until granted permission
It takes everything we have

to get here

We see this is everything there is

It looks different from here
than we thought it would

When it changes we'll be here to see it
No one can tell us

what we already know
but ourselves

Yet messages come in constantly
as clear as we think we are

to ourselves

It's never completely over

a pin drops
and we're here

                                                                4/3

EVERYTHING SHINES

You can't climb a mountain if your
feet are afraid

A gate left swinging in the air
can slam both ways

A narrow passageway can slowly
accommodate everyone

A canary could sing all day
and the bald not grow a single hair

When it's a matter of God or God's Name
we ought to think quite seriously

The smallest ant seems to know where
it's going yet so many end up in the

wrong place at the wrong time

After crossing a desert
any drink is refreshing

Johnny earned a string of A's
yet still feared for his life

The seraphim have only six or eight wings
yet a small number crowd the sky

Without a state of wonder
every bleak thing looks bleaker

We may have belief in the Reality of God
and still get away with things

inside His Gaze

God's not only partly God
but God completely

His reality in the creation is
complete completely

Everything shines with His Presence
and thinks itself beautiful

Everything shines in His Presence
and is beautiful

His Presence shines in everything

4/4

TIME TO WIND THIS DOWN

Perhaps it's time to wind this down

Fold up the backdrop panel by panel

Coil up the ropes and stow them behind
the engines idling at the sides

Collapse it all inside

Let the understudies in their
provisional costumes go

Pull up the tent pegs one by silver one
and kick the camp fires out

Lament the lost lovers
— they've left their marks

on our hearts

The bright children's faces
becoming like snowfall

The black night in front of which
their glittering flakes fall

The one star and all its
configured companions

spread out in the night

He'll fold up moon and stars Himself
He said

When the beasts have nowhere left
to go

and the fires gutter out

and shudders throb
through the rest of it

leaving only one left to leave it
having already left it

safe

4/8

NO TWO ALIKE OF ANYTHING

No two alike of anything are
completely alike

Everyone has been given a distinctive voice

Even perfectly mirroring each other
one creation has something of its own

distinct from its exact copy some tiny

isthmus of difference that if
extended out and magnified might be the

difference between say a hundred-petaled
rose and a hundred-and-one

petaled rose

And as everything moves or revolves in the
creation in search of its exact

opposite we change and transform from
nanosecond to nanosecond starting

out as a wild-eyed seeker with
electrified hair and at one

gesture we're now more moonlike and
the gracefulness of our

little finger on the right hand say
betrays a knowledge given to us we

didn't know we had

Open spaces evolve in all directions
and everywhere a waterfall of clarity

glistens through with its peaceful splashings
and exotic birds fly overhead

No landscape quite the same
though our eyes wander looking for the

tiniest unknown plant tendril that
turns out to be unique

that cures this new lump on my neck
I pray isn't cancerous

through whose phantom for
good or for ill flows

the same divine waterfall but whose

each bead of water is unlike
every other

and whose echoes on the rocks below
if magnified would out-melody and

out-crash Beethoven at his
most poignant

no singly sounded note
in time and space

quite the same as the same note sounded one
nanosecond earlier

and the Face of God like light through the
waterfall

silver note upon note
shimmering here

4/9

TRY

Try the razor sharp try the
strap to your right

Try horseback try tether-knot
try wild oats try wild rice try

every nothing that isn't wild try life itself
try leap into space try space light

for insular weather try life itself try
nothing left in the fridge try

nothing that isn't true itself
try the bridge over the River Conviction

Try side to side try to out-maneuver them
try the side of the building try

old dogs new tricks
(all tricks are new

— try them at home) try anything and
everything once before it turns black

try to keep a straight face try
laughing try weeping

Try the bend in a hairpin
turn in the road the

feather-light over a gorge

Try stepping lightly try stepping lively
try arms out straight try arms

at your sides
Try love no one dares not even

hidden in the dark
Try leaving everything unlocked try

every lock and key
try every door and when one opens

try to
give up trying and

enter

4/10

ROUGH COUNTRY

We've all been born in a rough country

Beast breath on the windows

Streets all end at the same place

Nights all come right down to earth
and fasten there

Backs of buildings where trains go
blasted houses blackened bricks

Hard alleys full of cars

It won't be so easy to get out of here
alive

Horse heads plow through the night
toward us

Beneficent horse heads
with eyes like God

This one can't have children
that one feels half-dead

This one forgets where she's going
that one knows and is afraid

The grind of atoms around and inside us
making these concrete pictures

and everywhere we hear that ocean sound
far from water

                                                4/15

AGAIN AND AGAIN

Speedometer readings from the
spirit world are literally

so out of this world incalculable by
world standards and closer to

flash-point instantaneous duplication in
one place that's actually

measurable displacement as if starting from
the base of Annapurna to immediate

peak arrival with no light-streaks or
movement of air

Makes even the evolution of lumbering dinosaurs over
century time-periods from

first low lizards to ultimate extinction go by in a
wink and onto other things as the

scattering comet-dust settles

Way inside the kernel of a single thought or
way inside the enormous cavern of a

single compassionate heartbeat surrounded by
aurora borealis nimbuses extending

infinitely outward may be the utter speed of
speedlessness that exists in this

shuddering domain of God's intimate
time of which we might be vouchsafed at

least a lightning glance-worth as

our entire lifetime speeds through all its
permutations skin-sheddings and every

emotional roller-coastering recapitulation
first little tiny gasps of air with

tiny finger-wrigglings to our long wrinkled
hands at the sides of our pillows as if in a

permanent gesture of prayer which it
is

Everything in the sky takes place this fast
everything on earth completely

out of our control is as momentous as a
tsunami tidal wave but not of tons of

raging water but rather spun golden
showers of sheer light pouring its

gallons and ghostly galleons over us
space by space in generating quick

spaceless dimensions of pure glory

so elementally pure as to put first true
smiles on our hearts that

bloom roseate petals onto our lips and
the light in our eyes that penetrates throughout

heaven's infinite precincts more remote than
even a thought is

The hand quicker than the eye
when both Hand and Eye are God's

and we at the zero middle point between
simply awed spectators watching

giant cloud greyhounds bound over hedges of
light into total invisibility faster than a

silvery blink that goes by so fast it
barely happens yet happens and

happens again

...and again

4/16 (North Carolina)

I ENTER THE CHAPEL OF MY FOREHEAD

1

I enter the chapel of my forehead in prostration
where it is cool and dark

Forehead against smooth boards eyes
closed hands at the sides of my head by my

ears where there's no sound

Body relaxed hips hinged

At ease and afloat in nowhereness
forever

2

The Madonna of the Beach
washed upright onto shore

starlight around her head

Whale song so distant it's unheard by us
two-leggeds

but some whales swoon or weep over those faraway
meaningful moans

Tips of peaks underwater where we are now
huddled like a chameleon squid in a grotto

just about to
poke out a pink and greeny-yellow body to

slink along searching for
news and a quick bite

All worlds in full throttle to the
utmost of their potential as New-Agers might say

and yet a pall of gloom over some
shouldering a child's coffin into a

new graveyard during a too-short
ceasefire soon to unravel

But here in the cool dome of prostration
all's peaceful and unworldly

The floor doesn't buckle or break open
Heaven extends from right here into

everywhere

4/17

MARRIED TO A MASS OF ATOMS

Married to a mass of whizzily multiplying
atoms inside and outside us from

birth forty days after inception
when the soul puts its blank face to the

window of the tiny forming being and starts to
look around getting used to its prison for

life to live out its life sentence

Married in a ceremony of angelic bells
and so many satin ribbons curling through

space floating ever-so-softly down inside the
womb but beyond the womb's dimensions

The long carpeted aisle and the trumpets
the bells pealing across town

Disney-like bluebirds with some of those
airborne satiny ribbons in their beaks

Married out of time but plopping us
into time with each ticking multiplication

each more delicate and incisive formation
those literal fingernails and toes

and those compass-like genitals
pointing us in one direction or another

or both

like an orchid in a box a
bride wears on her wrist

or like the sweat-ring around the
neck of the bridegroom working in a mill

becoming precisely ourselves married to
all this materiality out from soul's

star-wandering across galactic skies
and married ineluctably to

God throughout all this from
before the beginning to

beyond the end in a
continuum bright-blast ceremony of light

attended by all the antelope in
creation having bathed in silver waterfalls

as well as wheeling exotic birds of every
possible rainbow color making a sheer

pandemonium of uttermost silence
while we extend through fate's geographical paces

along the four-dimensional map
given us from

day one to day X
in God's GPS eyebeam that

follows us move by
move left turn by right turn

Married also to our unique destination and its
particular color and peculiar sensibility

breath by breath

before birth beyond death
to the ceremonial music of free-floating

galaxies barely rubbing each other's
harmonious or inharmonious circumferences

so gloriously soaring through space
with our awestruck faces

eyes peering out our unique portholes to gaze on
God's Paradise

where our marriage is truly
consummated first time

face to original face

THE ENVELOPE THAT CONTAINS THE MESSAGE

The envelope that contains the message
is also the message

and the hand that delivers the message
is also the message

and the body the hand is connected to
is also the message

and the face on the body and the
light or lack of light in the eyes of the

face is also the message

and the distance crossed from the
origin of the message seen or

unseen is also the message

until the clouds banked above in the
sky spell out the message

loud and clear

and the very fact of there
being a message also indicates

meaning that should
perk up our ears at our Sunday coffee

in the sunny kitchen or on the
sun-drenched mountaintop in a

cloak of wind enough to tear the
flesh off our bones

and yet when we read or hear such
messages in the ears or eyes of the

messengers we ourselves are
do we get the message after all or

crumple the sight or sound of it and
toss it aside like a house renovation flyer?

When our poor houses are so in
need of renovation

and the light that pours in through their chinks
an aquarium of glory in which we

might dwell where each
intake and outtake of breath

is the complete scroll unrolled and
rolled up again where the

message is imprinted and scintillates
like dazzling stars

4/22

A DRUNK JUGGLER

A drunk juggler lost his shoes and
came out barefoot

which was fine until he threw up torches
and the sparks scorched his toes

A sea lion claimed the entire beach to himself
and rolled around and lounged around

his huge rubbery bulk extending itself
as far as it could while the sea

sloshed against his finny elbows

Nothing really connects these two
except me and I

really don't want any part of it
I just started writing this poem at

2 in the morning to see if the heart's
secrets might be revealed perhaps a

word or phrase or even a
single stanza at a time

out of the dark forest of dense trees
owl hoots and strange

crackling sounds like someone
tiptoeing on sticks

All the world extends from
inside out of us

though we're in no way the Creator of it
but within us lie kingdoms

their rises and falls
scintillatingly outlined in both their

flowering and their ruin

each of us born like a lotus on the umbilical
stems of our mothers bobbing

just at the surface of the pond
in an ambiguous sunlight

Do we ever completely cut that cord
or rise completely out of the pond

except perhaps by evaporation
into the down-gazing sky?

The juggler shuffles off to find his shoes
all his torches suspended in midair

which has a nice look to it
at this point in the poem

and when the greedy sea lion gets tired of
rolling around on his territory and

falls asleep in the hot noonday sun
the whole herd moves in again and

a few bulls bigger than him
lie at his head and his tail

ready when he wakes up to
overpower him

Justice has been served
on this tiny planet

orbiting in space
and I'm going

back to sleep

4/25

HOW MANY CHANCES

How many chances do we get
before God lowers His great lids

over our affair

and the spindle we continually
twist around

evaporates into thin air?

We ride between stallions
heading for a cliff

that yawns gigantically below

and stop toes first at the outermost edge

How often do we stop before we
step out into thin air?

Dragged through our own swamps
to the drugged sound of swamp music

and a Lorelei languor lying over all
as we slide by

How many times do we come back from the
edged relieved it wasn't

this time the last time or the
time past the last time that's

beyond time our own time

run out?

O God that You
hold us close even in our

distance from You
each blood-beat a necklace

around a divine heart

Even knowing
our rampages

nearly never cease
yet Your Compassion

never ceases
to increase

4/26

AT SEAPOINT

At seapoint a window opens up
and you look out onto

outstretch upon outstretch of
water to where all details disappear and the

horizon is a tenuous line between
sea and sky

and sky may be sea you can
scan farther than your

eye can see

outstretch upon outstretch into God's
glorious seeing

and no seeing can see as God sees
as God sees all seeing

outstretch upon outstretch
beyond seeing

as only the heart
sees

4/27

EPITAPHS

The train slowed down so he could cross and
cross he did

One pasture remained uncultivated
so he's busy making up for

lost time

A cloud covers us all
one by one

You turn around and the
next moment we're gone

When we count everyone present
do we always forget to

count ourselves?

Off to play with the passed-on pets
keeping love alive

one life among so many

The smoke went up the chimney
and so did she

When the conversation stops

the air is still

How many lavender flowers dot the
mountainside how many

sunsets darken the hills?

Nothing's remembered so long as the
original colors don't change or fade

The essence has gone on to wear
other clothes

The last light hits the dark
like a strip of white

Things are getting serious
right about now

*Can you remember the
one about penguins?*

                                                5/2-3

FINDING THE RIGHT METAPHOR

> *"Then, what is life? I cried"*
> — Shelley *(last written words)*

Finding the right metaphor for the
all-of-it and our relationship to the

all-of-it has always been a monumental task
both personally and collectively

Are we here for just a moment on this
floating mountain in space

tying little farewell notes on everything and
everyone as we pass?

Is it a dining hall full of family trees in the
shape of people we're tied to by blood

gathering for as many courses as possible
and some hearty after-dinner songs

before lights out?

Each of us is a child of parents and
parents of children either physical or

the spirits of our inwardness revealed
in the half-light or spotlight of our

pause before our passing

Strangers on trains blabbing our
confessionals to seat mates we'll

never see again or
depth-diving into our souls and the

souls of beloveds like those Hawaiian
divers off cliffs with sunlit

grace and the up-splash of survival?

Is it undersea consciousness snorkeling with
multi-colored fish and color-changing polyps under rocks?

A shack on a lost island beach
between endless wave beats and the

loud jungle impenetrable and mysterious
behind us?

A horserace in endless ovals around
a track that leads nowhere?

An operation where we're
slowly divested of all our organs one by

one until purified of all earthly mortality?

Are we just outside death's door
with happy faces hearts on fire and

generous hugs for the other patients?

And are those heart-fires illuminating
us and all the other patients with true

warmth?

A circus where we walk out on a thin wire
alone in space our heavy balancing pole at

least holding us down

In a clearing with the other deer of the herd
standing heads high and ears twitching

alert to the quietest sound? The
tiniest twig-crack?

God's given us the latitudes of a
life span

rolling meadows and transparent brick walls
air in our lungs of epic proportions

or short frightened breaths as staccato as gunfire and as
fuzzy as tennis balls rotating in midair

The known frailties of our flesh
ignored for the most part

as our spirit realities keep tending
forward and forward and inwardly outward to

enter the shimmering
ice door once and for all

into divine chambers where we'll
meet all God's lovers in

spectacular landscapes in shivered
glitterings of angelic light

far from the hellish dark torments of our
repeated miscalculations

drinking in and passing around the inebriating
enchanted wine

of God's love

5/4

LOVE BOAT

Hedging our bets
going around the dynamited

building rather than through it

*(is all life such a building
evacuated — in the news —*

about to blow?)

Watching the flight patterns of birds
overhead

all our documents inside our
inside pockets for

quick retrieval

keeping our eye on the
finger that's being

kept on the button

when in fact it's really all
blue sky

but not just blue but
pellucid blue blue the blue of

light through emptiness
with cobalt depths

and sparkler textures

and a runway for angels
and they appear

musically arranged
those long blaring trumpets

foremost
louder than all the heavens

rung like a bell
but when played by angels

sound more like interweaving
waves of the sea

— High C

So really it's not such a
choice we make between

one or the other
but that we see the

purest blue behind the bustle
the coolest angelic behind the

boisterous

the message unfurled in plain sight
behind world news

and supreme as always
His Love

and we're on
His

Love Boat

5/5

GOLDEN BUCKET

I fly into sleep
like a golden bucket

THE MATCH THAT BECOMES A CONFLAGRATION

1

The match that became a conflagration
may not even strike and

flare into fire but sit parallel to all the
other matches in the box either

perfectly still as a stick with a
phosphor head or silently plotting itself

all aflame with inflammable rude
awakening

to catch a curtain hem on fire and
burn down a whole neighborhood

for simply being in its way

or a forest vertically celebrating its
upward urges now

burnt to the literal ground
squirrels shivering in fear in their

burrows and ants in a sudden
helter-skelter of activity looking for

shelter

while out in space a meteor shower
applauds its aplomb its bravado its

sheer flamey light

Behind the curtains of appearances the
flameless fires that generate illusory

movement flicker in silvery and molten
coppery approval

as a single match of potentially
infinite illumination

stirs in the inertness of its chemical makeup
and strikes itself against a

sand-papery surface

to a sudden symphony swelling into
thunderous color and sound

crack of sea-wrack and star-collision
car-wreck and alien trek across

illimitable distances

and in the flickering shadows cast across
nothingness a silhouette of

light bends to our desperate joy
in cooling mercy and smiles

as all things dance to His breath
and fold again almost indescribably

into our death

2

We carry our deaths around with us

He slouches in our dark doorways

She lights our cigarettes
even if we don't smoke

Tobogganing is only a part of it
skiing miraculously uphill

doesn't take us away from it
even as we see it purpling the

sunsets or sunrises over a
distant hill

Its windows are always open
its breezes blowing in

No end to its metaphors

that most urgent and

patient of lovers
of all the most true

who never leaves us for a moment
and takes us with it

when it goes
God bless its charmed heart

and its unprecedented
familiarity with every forgiven

tick and crack in us
loving us all the more for each of them

into whose cool embrace
we finally slide

our final prostration all those
other prostrations were

about

waiting to meet us
forehead to forehead

heart to heart
all souls

above all

Allah's bright
kaleidoscope

3

The matchsticks crinkle and
crumble away

everything contained in the possible
strike

struck dumb
struck down

the tiny length of a lifetime
with a phosphorous end

But we so wanted to light up the world
without cupping the flame

even just a corner where
others could come

and be
struck undumb

5/8-9

INDEX

A Drunk Juggler   208
A Pin Drop   181
A Pot of Ink   127
Advice on Aging   162
Again and Again   198
An Owl Flew Past   147
Are We Standing in One Place?   150
At Seapoint   213
Awakened by Nothing   162
Bird Count   142
Coat Ten Sizes Too Large   174
Death Can't Get You   69
Death Never Meets Us Halfway   108
Dumbfounded   140
Elephant Herd   33
Enter Me into the Great Adventure   54
Epitaphs   214
Every Wind   96
Everything Shines   187
Finding the Right Metaphor   216
First There Was Nothing   64
Forever   77
Fulsome Wind   18
Golden Bucket   223
Good Horse Good Horse   176
Green And Blue Marble-Sized Sphere   52
How Can We Not Admire   20

How Many Chances   211
I Can't Prove God Exists   88
I Enter the Chapel of My Forehead   201
If Your Vessel Springs a Leak   82
If a Giant Ocean Liner   154
In This World   19
Is It Too Late to Wonder   179
It Starts Out Small   66
It's Not to Do   139
Last Things   163
Love Boat   220
Married to a Mass of Atoms   203
Mouse Hole   79
Multilingual Alabaster Candelabra   99
Music of the Spheres   156
Navigate That!   60
No Second Face   116
No Two Alike of Anything   191
Not Mine   28
Now We are a Norwegian   172
Of Course the Essence of it All   85
One Note Sounds   72
Poem in the First Person   21
Rough Country   196
Saffron Edge and Lavender Center   114
Sam the Big River   102
Sharper and Sharper   160
Silks from Persia Gems from Yemen   133
Sound Advice   131

Such a Difference   62
Sumptuous Sunken Pool   48
Talking to God   75
The Boats   44
The Bus of Bones   98
The Call That Takes Us There   73
The Envelope that Contains the Message   206
The Fish That Swallowed Jonah   58
The Fortress Looked Down   178
The Gorgeousness of the Shadow   41
The Hawk Flies Past Midnight   24
The Hourglass   94
The Magic in a Glance   120
The Match that Became a Conflagration   224
The Match that Becomes a Conflagration   17
The Miraculous Scaffoldings   90
The Most Beautiful Ship   124
The Power of a Body of Water   167
The Salient Thing About Sainthood   100
The Strike to Watch   105
The World   38
The World Went Away   29
They Try to Approach   143
Time Slides By   135
Time to Wind This Down   189
Tiny Scholars on Mountainpeaks   51
Took a Deep Breath   92
Try   194

We Live in an Exquisite World   145
We're a Sensitive Bunch   152
When Seraphim Fly Overhead   122
When the Circus Comes to Town   46
While in This World   112
Wine Poured Out   26
You Take a Picture   169

ABOUT THE AUTHOR

Born in 1940 in Oakland, California, Daniel Abdal-Hayy Moore had his first book of poems, *Dawn Visions*, published by Lawrence Ferlinghetti of City Lights Books, San Francisco, in 1964, and the second in 1972, *Burnt Heart/Ode to the War Dead*. He created and directed *The Floating Lotus Magic Opera Company* in Berkeley, California in the late 60s, and presented two major productions, *The Walls Are Running Blood*, and *Bliss Apocalypse*. He became a Sufi Muslim in 1970, performed the Hajj in 1972, and lived and traveled throughout Morocco, Spain, Algeria and Nigeria, landing in California and publishing *The Desert is the Only Way Out*, and *Chronicles of Akhira* in the early 80s (Zilzal Press). Residing in Philadelphia since 1990, in 1996 he published *The Ramadan Sonnets* (Jusoor/City Lights), and in 2002, *The Blind Beekeeper* (Jusoor/Syracuse University Press). He has been the major editor for a number of works, including *The Burdah* of Shaykh Busiri, translated by Hamza Yusuf, and the poetry of Palestinian poet, Mahmoud Darwish, translated by Munir Akash. He is also widely published on the worldwide web: *The American Muslim,* and his own website *www.ecstaticxchange.com*. He has been poetry editor for *Seasons Journal, Islamica Magazine,* a 2010 translation by Munir Akash of *State of Siege*, by Mahmoud Darwish (Syracuse University Press), and *The Prayer of the Oppressed*, by Imam Muhammad Nasir al-Dar'i, translated by Hamza Yusuf. In 2011, 2012 and 2014 he was a winner of the Nazim Hikmet Prize for Poetry. In 2013 he won an American Book Award, and in 2013 and 2014 was listed among The 500 Most Influential Muslims for his poetry. *The Ecstatic Exchange Series* is bringing out the extensive body of his works of poetry (a complete list of published works on page 2).

POETIC WORKS
by Daniel Abdal-Hayy Moore

Published and Unpublished
Dawn Visions (published by City Lights, 1964)
Burnt Heart/Ode to the War Dead (published by City Lights, 1972)
This Body of Black Light Gone Through the Diamond (printed by Fred Stone, Cambridge, Mass, 1965)
On The Streets at Night Alone (1965?)
All Hail the Surgical Lamp (1967)
States of Amazement (1970)

Abdallah Jones and the Disappearing-Dust Caper (published by The Ecstatic Exchange/Crescent Series, 2006)
'Ala ud-Deen and the Magic Lamp (published by The Ecstatic Exchange, 2011)
The Chronicles of Akhira (1981) (published by Zilzal Press with Typoglyphs by Karl Kempton, 1986; (published in Sparrow on the Prophet's Tomb by The Ecstatic Exchange, 2009)
Mouloud (1984) (A Zilzal Press chapbook, 1995; published in Sparrow on the Prophet's Tomb by The Ecstatic Exchange, 2009)
The Crown of Creation (1984) (published by The Ecstatic Exchange, 2012)
The Look of the Lion (The Parabolas of Sight) (1984)
The Desert is the Only Way Out (completed 4/21/84) (Zilzal Press chapbook, 1985)
Atomic Dance (1984) (am here books, 1988)
Outlandish Tales (1984)
Awake as Never Before (12/26/84) (Zilzal Press chapbook, 1993)
Glorious Intervals (1/1/85) (Zilzal Press chapbook, ?)
Long Days on Earth/Book I (1/28 – 8/30/85)
Long Days on Earth/Book II (Hayy Ibn Yaqzan)
Long Days on Earth/Book III (1/22/86)
Long Days on Earth/Book IV (1986)
The Ramadan Sonnets (Long Days on Earth/Book V) (5/9 – 6/11/86) (published by Jusoor/City Lights Books, 1996) (republished as Ramadan Sonnets by The Ecstatic Exchange, 2005)
Long Days on Earth/Book VI (6-8/30/86)
Holograms (9/4/86 – 3/26/87)
History of the World (The Epic of Man's Survival) (4/7 – 6/18/87)

Exploratory Odes (6/25 – 10/18/87)
The Man at the End of the World (11/11 – 12/10/87)
The Perfect Orchestra (3/30 – 7/25/88)(published by The Ecstatic Exchange, 2009)
Fed from Underground Springs (7/30 – 11/23/88)
Ideas of the Heart (11/27/88 – 5/5/89)
New Poems (scattered poems, out of series, from 3/24 – 8/9/89)
Facing Mecca (5/16 – 11/11/89) (published by The Ecstatic Exchange, 2014)
A Maddening Disregard for the Passage of Time (11/17/89 – 5/20/90) (published by The Ecstatic Exchange, 2009)
The Heart Falls in Love with Visions of Perfection (6/15/90 – 6/2/91)
Like When You Wave at a Train and the Train Hoots Back at You (Farid's Book) (6/11 – 7/26/91) (published by The Ecstatic Exchange, 2008)
Orpheus Meets Morpheus (8/1/91– 3/14/92)
The Puzzle (3/21/92 – 8/17/93)(published by The Ecstatic Exchange, 2011)
The Greater Vehicle (10/17/93 – 4/30/94)
A Hundred Little 3-D Pictures (5/14/94 – 9/11/95) (published by The Ecstatic Exchange, 2013)
The Angel Broadcast (9/29 – 12/17/95)
Mecca/Medina Time-Warp (12/19/95 – 1/6/96) (published as a Zilzal Press chapbook, 1996)(published in Sparrow on the Prophet's Tomb, 2009)
Miracle Songs for the Millennium (1/20 – 10/16/96)(published by The Ecstatic Exchange, 2014)
The Blind Beekeeper (11/15/96 – 5/30/97) (published 2002 by Jusoor/ Syracuse University Press)
Chants for the Beauty Feast (6/3 – 10/28/97)(published by The Ecstatic Exchange, 2011
You Open a Door and it's a Starry Night (10/29/97 – 5/23/98) (published by The Ecstatic Exchange, 2009)
Salt Prayers (5/29 – 10/24/98) (published by The Ecstatic Exchange, 2005)
Some (10/25/98 – 4/25/99) (published by The Ecstatic Exchange, 2014)
Flight to Egypt (5/1 – 5/16/99)
I Imagine a Lion (5/21 – 11/15/99) (published by The Ecstatic Exchange, 2006)
Millennial Prognostications (11/25/99 – 2/2/2000) (published by the Ecstatic Exchange, 2009)
Shaking the Quicksilver Pool (2/4 – 10/8/2000) (published by The Ecstatic Exchange, 2009)

Blood Songs (10/9/2000 – 4/3/2001)(Published by The Ecstatic Exchange, 2012)
The Music Space (4/10 – 9/16/2001) (published by The Ecstatic Exchange, 2007)
Where Death Goes (9/20/2001 – 5/1/2002) (published by The Ecstatic Exchange, 2009)
The Flame of Transformation Turns to Light (99 Ghazals Written in English) (5/14 – 8/21/2002) (published by The Ecstatic Exchange, 2007)
Through Rose-Colored Glasses (7/22/2002 – 1/15/2003) (published by The Ecstatic Exchange, 2007)
Psalms for the Broken-Hearted (1/22 – 5/25/2003) (published by The Ecstatic Exchange, 2006)
Hoopoe's Argument (5/27 – 9/18/03)
Love is a Letter Burning in a High Wind (9/21 – 11/6/2003) (published by The Ecstatic Exchange, 2006)
Laughing Buddha/Weeping Sufi (11/7/2003 – 1/10/2004) (published by The Ecstatic Exchange, 2005)
Mars and Beyond (1/20 – 3/29/2004) (published by The Ecstatic Exchange, 2005)
Underwater Galaxies (4/5 – 7/21/2004) (published by The Ecstatic Exchange, 2007)
Cooked Oranges (7/23/2004 – 1/24/2005) (published by The Ecstatic Exchange, 2007)
Holiday from the Perfect Crime (1/25 – 6/11/2005) (published by The Ecstatic Exchange, 2011)
Stories Too Fiery to Sing Too Watery to Whisper (6/13 – 10/24/2005) (published by The Ecstatic Exchange, 2014)
Coattails of the Saint (10/26/2005 – 5/10/2006) (published by The Ecstatic Exchange, 2006)
In the Realm of Neither (5/14/2006 – 11/12/06) (published by The Ecstatic Exchange, 2008)
Invention of the Wheel (11/13/06 – 6/10/07)(published by The Ecstatic Exchange, 2010)
The Sound of Geese Over the House (6/15 – 11/4/07)(published by The Ecstatic Exchange, 2015)
The Fire Eater's Lunchbreak (11/11/07 – 5/19/2008) (published by The Ecstatic Exchange, 2008)
Sparks Off the Main Strike (5/24/2008 – 1/10/2009)(published by The Ecstatic

Exchange, 2010)
Stretched Out on Amethysts (1/13 – 9/17/2009)(published by The Ecstatic Exchange, 2010)
The Throne Perpendicular to All that is Horizontal (9/18/09 – 1/25/10) (published by The Ecstatic Exchange, 2014)
In Constant Incandescence (2/10 – 8/13/10) (published by The Ecstatic Exchange, 2011)
The Caged Bear Spies the Angel (8/30/10 – 3/6/11)(published by The Ecstatic Exchange, 2010)
This Light Slants Upward (3/7 – 10/13/11)
Ramadan is Burnished Sunlight (part of This Light Slants Upward, published separately by The Ecstatic Exchange, 2011)
The Match That Becomes a Conflagration (10/14/11 – 5/9/12) (published by The cstatic Exchange, 2016)
Down at the Deep End (5/10 – 8/3/12) (published by The Ecstatic Exchange, 2012)
Next Life (8/9/12 – 2/12/13) (published by The Ecstatic Exchange, 2013)
The Soul's Home (2/13 – 10/8/13) (published by The Ecstatic Exchange, 2014)
Eternity Shimmers & Time Holds its Breath (10/10/13 – 1/27/14) (published by The Ecstatic Exchange, 2014)
He Comes Running (part of Eternity Shimmers, published as an Ecstatic Exchange Chapbook, 2014)
The Sweet Enigma of it All (1/29 – 6/18/14) (published by The Ecstatic Exchange, 2014)
Let Me See Diamonds Everywhere I Look (6/18/14 – 1/15/15)
With Every Breath (1/18/15 --)
White Noise in This World Silver in the Next (5/1 -- 10/17/15) (published by The Ecstatic Exchange, 2015)

www.ingramcontent.com/pod-product-compliance
Lightning Source LLC
Chambersburg PA
CBHW032040150426
43194CB00006B/364